Taishō Kimono

"КАМЕЛІЯ„

ФОРМОЗСКІЙ

Jan Dees

Taishō Kimono
Speaking of Past and Present

Photography by
Michiel Elsevier Stokmans

SKIRA

Cover
Majestic white *hōō*
Woman's *furisode*
(cat. 6, detail)

Spine
'A study of elegance'
Man's *haori*
(cat. 61, detail)

Back cover
Cranes flying above the sea
Woman's *furisode,* part of a set
(cat. 7b)

Frontspiece
"Camellia" geisha
Promotion postcard for Formosa tea
(*ca.* 1910). Author's collection

Design
Marcello Francone

Editorial coordination
Vincenza Russo

Editing
Timothy Stroud

Layout
Serena Parini

First published in Italy in 2009 by
Skira Editore S.p.A.
Palazzo Casati Stampa
via Torino 61
20123 Milano
Italy
www.skira.net

Printed and bound in Italy. First edition
ISBN: 978-88-572-0011-8

Distributed in North America
by Rizzoli International Publications,
Inc., 300 Park Avenue South, New York,
NY 10010, USA.
Distributed elsewhere in the world
by Thames and Hudson Ltd.,
181A High Holborn,
London WC1V 7QX, United Kingdom.

Contents

Preface and Aims

Taishō Kimono brings together two of my longtime interests: Asian textiles and Japanese art.

Being part of our colonial past, Indonesian textiles were to some extent familiar to most people in the Netherlands until recently. Up to the 1960s, ikats from the island of Sumba could be commonly found as the decoration of the chimney or the cover of the divan in many a Dutch home, and Ambonese women, who had fled their native country following Indonesia's independence, could often be seen wearing a batik sarong and *kebaya* blouse. However, the astonishing variety of Indonesian textiles was certainly not common knowledge. In my case, acquaintance with this wonderful world took place in the mid-1980s at an overview exhibition in the ethnographic Nusantara Museum in Delft, where cloths from all over the archipelago were shown. Several outstanding auctions of Indonesian textiles during the late 1980s lured me into becoming a collector. The coarse handspun ikats of Lamalera, the gorgeous *songket* weavings of Palembang and the batiks from Java's north coast all held their own beauty, created by the skilled hands of women. Journeys to Sarawak enabled me to see old Iban women making intricate *ikat* weavings without using any kind of pattern. From the books I learned that numerous motifs and techniques had come to Indonesia through trade from India, for example with the famous *patola* cloths. In the Gujarat town of Pattan, two workshops for the manufacture of the double-*ikat patola* appeared to be still operating. In the same house where Alfred Bühler had assembled much of the material for his two-volume book on *patola*, one can still get a closer understanding of the efforts and skills that are required for the creation of such masterpieces.

Gradually my collection began to include Asian textiles from a wider area. When other interests became more pressing, however, my South-East Asian textiles were accepted as a donation by the Nusantara Museum, where my fascination had begun. The competing interest concerned Japanese art.

In 1975, long before our acquaintance with Indonesian textiles, my partner and I had started collecting Japanese lacquer. During the 1980s Japanese art became a hype in the Western world, induced by the economic miracle in the land of the rising sun. I became involved in the organisation of a few exhibitions and started writing on the subject. When prices for Japanese lacquer soared to such a degree that we were no longer able to buy what we really liked, we decided to sell our small collection. I expected that my fascinating hobby would soon be gone too, and turned to collect Indonesian and South-East Asian textiles instead. Unexpectedly, the international network of collectors, curators and dealers proved to be steady, and all the time new opportunities arose to conduct studies on lacquer topics, both in Europe, the USA and Japan. The focus of my pressing pursuit became Japanese lacquer art of the period between 1890 and 1950. However, during trips to Japan I often came across beautiful textiles from that same period, and I felt regularly tempted to buy one or two pieces. In later years acquisitions were made at a faster pace through internet and email contacts with dealers. Once I had completed my dissertation on Japanese lacquer, the urge to present the textile collection at an exhibition and in a book began to burgeon. My partner René van der Star had organised two exhibitions on ethnic jewellery in the Rotterdam Kunsthal and concomitantly published two books. The director of the Kunsthal immediately accepted the proposal for an exhibition on Taishō kimono, and Skira was ready to publish the book.

Taishō Kimono does not offer a scholarly approach to the subject. Although the introductory essays present the background of the period in general and of Japanese dress in particular, this is not the most significant part. What this book aims to highlight are the individual textiles: their shapes, fabrics, decoration techniques and motifs. In this way the garments themselves tell the story of Japanese traditional dress during the late Meiji, Taishō, and early Shōwa eras. The word Taishō was chosen as *pars pro toto* for the period as a whole since the liberal culture during the short reign of the Taishō emperor (1912–1926) is so strongly associated with the typical amalgam of tradition and modernity, which can also be observed in the textiles.

The book wants to make two statements: one on the significance of traditional decorations found on Taishō kimono, and the other on the fascinating story-telling designs on men's kimono.

In recent years a number of publications have focused on modernity and modernism in Japanese dress during the 1920s and 1930s, and this is indeed one of the major attractions of the period. However, it is only half the story. Just as in Japanese art in general, Taishō dress also had strongly traditional traits. After the period of uncritical Westernisation during the early Meiji period, the beginning of the twentieth century celebrated the revival of 'Japaneseness' parallel to the emergence of modernity. Many kimono were decorated with traditional or even nostalgic designs of court ladies, samurai, geisha, theatre, autumn grasses, cranes, Gods of Good Fortune, etc. These motifs seem to reflect the regained national pride after the remarkable development of the country from its backward position in the mid-nineteenth century to a powerful nation in the early twentieth century. Having seen thousands of kimono from this period, one gets the impression that traditional decorations far outnumbered the modern designs.

The second statement concerns men's kimono, which have been underexposed in most publications, but are as appealing as women's kimono, though for different reasons. Men's kimono were certainly less eye-catching and never flamboyant, but their designs in subdued colours appear to be extremely interesting once attempts are made to decode their meaning. The hidden decorations on the linings of jackets and on under-kimono were hardly ever shown in public. Men probably selected images of the tea ceremony, theatre, Buddhist subjects, horse racing, baseball or war because they matched their interests, sentiments or convictions, and perhaps as an affirmation of their identity. Men's dress covers the narrative pictorial elements of fashion.

Acknowledgements

Decoding the meaning of designs was not always easy. In this respect my long-time interest in Japanese art paid off, since many motifs could be read like a rebus. Other images proved too difficult, but were explained to me by knowledgeable friends: Henk en Arendie Herwig (no. 76), Ms Seo Chiaki (nos. 43, 51, 52), Tokugo Uchida (nos. 46, 55), Ms Wada Yuka (no. 59) and

Yoshikawa Hideki (nos. 61, 62), whereas some designs remained mysteries.

Several people and institutions assisted in providing important illustrations to elucidate a textile technique, a design, a historical feature or just the spirit of the time. For this I would like to thank Henk en Arendie Herwig, Eric van den Ing, the Koninklijk Huis Archief in the Hague, the National Diet Library in Tokyo, the Nishijin Industrial Textile Association (Ms. Nakagawa) in Kyoto, Steve Sundberg, the Takashimaya Historical Museum in Osaka, Christiaan Uhlenbeck, Robert Uterwijk, Mr and Ms Wessels and the Wiebrens collection.

Having done a similar project twice before, my partner René van der Star made the present undertaking much easier, since we already had access to Wim Pijbes – until recently the energetic director of Kunsthal but in the meantime appointed head-director of the Rijksmuseum – and his efficient staff. Charlotte van Lingen curated the exhibition. Equally important was the acquaintance with Michiel Elsevier Stokmans, the extremely skilled head of the photography department of Christie's Amsterdam, who knows art photography inside out. In a series of Saturdays, our living room was converted into a photographic studio, where Michiel digitally recorded what I had been ironing in the days before. The third partner in the tried and tested formula was Francesco Baragiola of the Milan-based art publisher Skira, which produced the book as a companion to the exhibition. It was a great pleasure to cooperate with Vincenza Russo and her editorial team.

Jan Dees

The Kimono in Modern Japan 1868–1937

It was only during the first decade of the twentieth century that the kimono came to be regarded as Japan's national dress by the Japanese themselves. Foreigners had admired the elegant traditional dress ever since the opening of the country after the 1868 Meiji Restoration, but in those days the Japanese were infatuated with novelties from the West. Accounts by early foreign residents, such as the American Edward Sylvester Morse and the Englishman Basil Hall Chamberlain, lamented the disappearing interest in kimono in favour of Western dress.[1] Traditional modes of life in general were vanishing at such an alarming pace that several authors declared Old Japan dead and gone by 1890. This was the result of an unprecedented modernisation of the country during the first half of the Meiji period (1868–1912). Once this goal had been achieved and Japan had gained a significant position in the world, the emerging nationalism and patriotism brought renewed interest in traditional values and native dress. Increasing prosperity among large segments of the population subsequently caused an upswing in kimono fashion during the 1920s and 1930s.

Dress during the Meiji era

In 1867, following 250 years of seclusion from the outside world, the declining regime of the Tokugawa shoguns broke down. The collapse was due to the intrusion by the USA and other Western countries, which demanded trade concessions and other privileges (the Unequal Treaties). Backward Japan felt threatened by the thought of being reduced to a semi-colonial status, as had occurred to China after the Opium War (1839–1842). A group of feudal lords (*daimyō*) from

western Japan sensed their chances and violently overturned the Tokugawa clan in central Japan. At the end of this civil war the emperor was reinstated as head of the country: the 1868 Meiji Restoration. An oligarchy of young and ambitious samurai from the western domains tried to resist the threat of the foreign nations by a vigorous unification and modernisation process. During the first decades of the Meiji era they succeeded in forging a unified nation out of the compartmentalised social and political structure of the Tokugawa era (1600–1868). The feudal domains were abolished, and so were the four traditional classes. Samurai, farmers, artisans and merchants all became commoners. The school system was much improved and a conscript army was formed to replace the samurai. The introduction of a single currency, the yen, stimulated the development of a national economy. Eventually a constitution was promulgated (1889), which provided the young nation with a parliament and suffrage, although only 1% of the population was entitled to vote – all men, of course.

Another way of resisting Western pressure and exploitation was – paradoxically – the propagation of a Western mode of life. Young men were sent abroad to study the nature of the West, whereas European and American experts were hired to teach in Japan. Under the slogan 'civilisation and enlightenment' (*bummei kaika*), coined by the influential journalist Fukuzawa Yukichi (1835–1901) (fig. 1), railways were constructed and horse trolleys appeared in the streets of the cities, universities were founded and newspapers published.

Traditional dress was regarded as old-fashioned, and for men considered effeminate.[2] Dress regulations at court dictated Western dress as early as 1872. Upper-class men and women in the big cities followed suit in order to socialise more easily with foreigners (fig. 2). The Deer Cry Pavilion (*Rokumeikan*) was the place where the Japanese elite and Westerners met (fig. 3). The building had been designed by the British architect Josiah Conder (1852–1920) in 1883. Balls and garden parties were organised, one could play billiards or enjoy European classical music. The sole purpose of this all was, from the government's point of view, to become regarded as 'equal' and 'civilised' by the West in order to escape exploitation and to reverse the privileges as laid down in the Unequal Treaties. Soon most government employees were required to wear uniform or Western dress as well. Basil Chamberlain remarked:

"The undignified billy-cocks and pantaloons of the West are slowly but surely supplanting the picturesque, aristocratic-looking native garb, – a change for which the Government is mainly responsible, as it obliges almost all officials to wear European dress when on duty, and of course the inferior classes ape their betters. Nor have women, though naturally more conservative, been altogether able to resist the radicalism of their time and country."[3]

The government boosted economic development in many fields. Silk products became the mainstay of export for decades, and propelled Japan's economy onto the world market. Already before the Restoration Japan had benefited from the outbreak of the silkworm disease *pebrine* in the French silkworm factories in 1854. Only when Louis Pasteur had discovered parasitic infections as the cause of the epidemic more than ten years later and a remedy had been found, was the French production gradually restored. Until 1873, a large part of the total Japanese export therefore consisted – next to raw silk – of silkworm eggs.[4] By the turn of the century, Japan had become the world's leading silk producer (fig. 4). Apart from the raw material, silk fabrics became an increasingly important commodity for the overseas and home markets.

The imperial capital Kyoto had been the centre of silk weaving and dyeing for centuries, and the court was a major customer. In 1869, however, the imperial capital was moved to Tokyo. This meant a heavy blow for the economy of the ancient city. A succession of disastrous harvests during the end of the Tokugawa period had already

driven numerous weavers of the weaving quarter Nishijin out of their jobs, and now the departure of the court caused another sharp fall in the demand for luxury fabrics. To reverse the decline, the governor of Kyoto sent the merchant Sakura Tsuneshichi and the weavers Inoue Ihee and Yoshida Chushichi to Lyon in order to study modern European weaving technology (fig. 5).[5] In 1873, they brought back the jacquard loom, which was going to revolutionise Nishijin's production of both hand-woven and machine-woven brocade silk. The new single-operator loom replaced the large traditional loom that had required, apart from the weaver, one or two assistants. As a result, Kyoto continued to be the centre of *nishiki* brocade for another century.

In 1875 a group of Nishijin artisans was sent to Europe to study the newly invented chemical dyes. Soon these dyes would find application in a technique of direct stencil-dyeing with a mixture of dyes and rice paste, which was developed by Hirose Jisuke in 1879. This new technology, adapted to the local circumstances, innovated the silk industry in Japan, and would enable large scale production when traditional dress began to be re-appreciated after the turn of the century.

The modernisation of daily life was primarily a feature of the big cities. In rural Japan most people were still clad in handspun cotton garments, mostly dyed with indigo and decorated with *ikat* or tie-dye patterns (fig. 6). But also in the big cities ordinary women continued to dress traditionally, often in simple striped kimono. Modernity was for men, tradition for women.

2. Japanese *fin de siècle* lady dressed in lace. Author's collection

3. The Rokumeikan Club (built in 1883), where the Japanese elite and Westerners met. National Diet Library Website

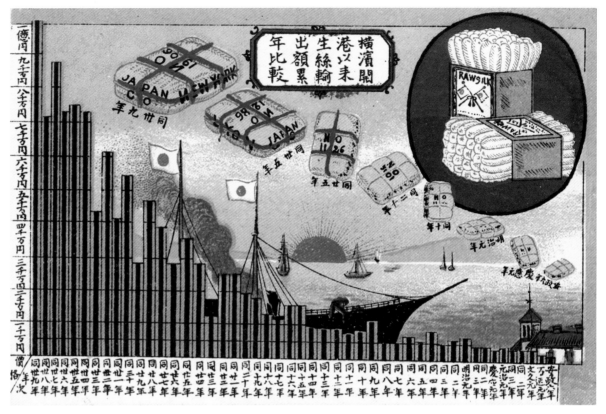

4. Postcard showing the increasing export value of raw silk through the port of Yokohama between 1859 and 1906 (from right to left). Author's collection

5. Delegation of weaving experts, who came back from a study trip to Lyon with the jacquard loom in 1873. Nishijin Textile Industrial Association, Kyoto

After the height of the Western fever in the 1880s, a conservative trend began to prevail in society. Many Japanese started to realise that Westernisation had gone too far. A reflection on the nation's own identity was considered necessary. The popular slogan 'a rich country, a strong army' (*fukoku kyōhei*) demonstrates the rising nationalism. Tension created with regard to the domination over Korea ('the dagger pointed at the heart of Japan') resulted in the Sino-Japanese War of 1894–1895 and the Russo-Japanese War of 1904–1905. Victory in both wars greatly boosted nationalism and patriotism. Fifty years after the traumatic intrusion by the West, Japan had become a powerful nation itself with Formosa as a colony, Korea as a protectorate and extensive interests in Manchuria. The Western craze subsided and was replaced by a proud feeling of self-respect. Foreign advisors were no longer necessary. The traditional arts, which had been mainly export-oriented in the early years of Meiji, started to flourish again.

Western dress was no longer particularly desirable, although men did not return *en masse* to traditional dress as upper-class women did.

A typical late Meiji phenomenon in women's dress was the *hakama* skirt, which developed from the pleaded *hakama* trousers men used to wear during the Tokugawa era. Women started wearing these *hakama* skirts over their kimono and in combination with a jacket (*haori*), which had also been a man's garment so far. This combination became the school uniform for girls.

Traditional kimono also regained their popularity, but for practical reasons the trailing hems were avoided by tucking in any excessive length under the sash (*obi*) (fig. 7). Initially, many kimono were only decorated on a limited area at the hems, often with detailed landscapes.

Top quality kimono even began to enter the realm of changing fashion. Remarkably, it was not the internationally prevailing Art Nouveau, but a style from Japan's past that dominated the fashion. The last decade of the Meiji era witnessed a revival of the kimono designs from the Genroku period (1688–1704): extremely large motifs in two-dimensional representations (cat. 1, 2).[6] Whereas the original style had reflected the confidence and wealth of the new merchant class of the Tokugawa period, its revival during the years following 1906 expressed the self-esteem of the rising world power.

The budding modern department stores, such as Mitsukoshi, Takashimaya, Matsuya and Daimaru, played leading roles in the revival of the kimono. Mitsukoshi in Tokyo even opened a design department for kimono, which employed students and graduates of the Nihonga (Japanese painting style) department of the Tokyo Art School (fig. 8). Takashimaya in Kyoto entertained strong connections with leading *nihonga* painters from the ancient capital.[7] Not only were artists like Kōno Bairei (1844–95), Takeuchi Seihō (1864–1942) and Kamisaka Sekka (1866–1942) hired to design textiles, they were also involved in the development of marketing tools such as

6. During the Meiji era most common people continued to wear traditional dress. Postcard, author's collection

posters, postcards and the covers of company magazines.[8] At the same time, the department stores started modernising their interiors. In some stores, like Takashimaya in Kyoto, it was no longer necessary to remove one's shoes before entering, and here and there kimono were exhibited in glass showcases (fig. 9). These adaptations were meant to stimulate the perception that kimono were fashion items.

In addition to the department stores, numerous specialist kimono dealers (*gofukuten*) continued to operate. These retailers often advertised their items by handing out lithograph bills to their best customers (fig. 10). Customers could select fabrics displayed for them on the *tatami* mats or choose designs from design books (*hinagatabon*). Numerous of these books from the turn of the century – both by well-known artists and anonymous designers – have survived, and testify to the renewed interest in kimono (fig. 11).

Thus the kimono came to be regarded as Japan's national dress by the Japanese themselves in the first decade of the twentieth century, but only for women.

Taishō culture

After the death of the Meiji emperor in 1912, his son Yoshihito ascended the throne. He named the period of his reign Taishō or Great Righteousness (1912–26). During the subsequent fifteen years a liberal and cosmopolitan culture emerged, especially in the metropolises, and on the political level a modern democracy started to

take shape. However, the period was also tormented by major incidents and a huge catastrophe. Increasing prosperity, the bent for modernity and the catastrophe all had an impact on the development of dress.

During the Great War, Japan's economy boomed due to slumping industrial output in Europe. An extensive working class of both men and women came into being, and large segments of the population benefited from the increasing prosperity.

Once the Great War was over and the League of Nations founded, a wave of international liberalism flooded the world, a climate from which Japanese democracy benefited. Political parties got their chance. In 1918 Hara Kei was the first commoner to be appointed Prime Minister, and in 1925 universal manhood suffrage was introduced. This period, known as Taishō Democracy, lasted until 1932.

At a more basic level, society became more democratic due to a higher level of education, increasing social mobility and vastly expanded transportation and communication, resulting in the creation of a mass culture.[9]

In spite of the spirit of optimism, the period of Taishō Democracy was basically unstable. Sharply dropping rice prices during the post-war depression caused serious unrest among farmers in 1921, and in that same year the Prime Minister, Hara Kei, was assassinated. There were scandals of corruption involving politicians and businessmen, and the relationship between political

7. Hand-coloured postcard showing a girl in kimono (1910). Under the sash, the fold for adapting the excess length of the kimono can be observed. Author's collection

8. Poster *Genroku bijin* designed by Yamada Shūho for Mitsukoshi in 1911. Takashimaya Historical Museum, Osaka

9. The showroom of Mitsukoshi, where kimono were displayed in glass showcases as a novelty (1911). National Diet Library Website

parties and business conglomerates (*zaibatsu*) became a matter of suspicion and debate.

Even the earth was unstable. On 1 September 1923 the Tokyo-Yokohama region – the Kantō plain – was heavily struck by an earthquake, which was followed by catastrophic fires (fig. 12). Some 140,000 people lost their lives and three-quarters of the buildings were destroyed or severely damaged.

The reconstruction of the city under the direction of Gotō Shinpei (1857–1929) was remarkably swift. The moats that had provided transport by boat were replaced by major avenues, local railways and the subway. Private railways connected the city centre to the newly built suburbs with partly Western-style housing. Ginza became the showplace of the city. In their flashiest Western clothing, the *mobo* and *moga* (modern boy and modern girl) paraded the streets, sometimes walking hand in hand. Giant department stores, where it was no longer necessary to remove one's shoes to protect the *tatami* mats, opened the doors of their brand-new buildings (fig. 13). Mitsukoshi even had an elevator, fire sprinklers and an air filtration system. Shopping and window-shopping became favourite pastimes. Cafés with attractive waitresses sprouted up 'like bamboo shoots after a rain'.[10] A consumer culture for ever larger urban masses took shape. By 1930 Tokyo was a much more modern and cosmopolitan metropolis than it had been before the catastrophe. Post-earthquake Taishō was a much younger culture than Meiji had been. Like everywhere else in the world, all kinds of entertainments flourished. Taishō is often characterised as

cosmopolitan, private, self-cultivating, and consumerist, in contrast to Meiji's traits: nationalist, public, self-sacrificing, and productionist.[11]

The position of women was highly topical in newspapers and magazines. The ideal of 'good wives and wise mothers' (*ryōsai kenbo*) made way for the desire of working outside the home as a teacher, a nurse or an office employee, and participating in social life: 'the new woman' (*atarashii onna*).[12] Young women dreamed of marriage based on love, and more militant women organised themselves to advocate birth control and women's suffrage. The suffragettes almost achieved their goal in 1931, when the House of Representatives passed the bill giving women the right to vote, but the House of Peers refused to give its approval.

Although in the past decade many publications on Taishō Culture have given a biased portrayal of modernity and modernism, this era also had strong traditional traits. After the Western craze of early Meiji, nostalgia for the samurai and court ladies, and for the traditional arts and crafts were equally part of the mood of the new time, not only as remnants of the past, but as vital and essential elements of the Taishō Culture. Japanese and Western elements, tradition and modernity fused into that peculiar Taishō amalgam.

Revealing in this respect was the survey carried out by Kon Wajirō on the main street of Ginza among more than one thousand men and women in the summer of 1925. Whereas he found that only 33% of the men were wearing kimono, 99% of the women wore traditional Japanese dress (fig. 14).[13] The 'modern girl' and the 'new woman' (*atarashii onna*) may have been powerful symbols on posters and covers of magazines, but the reality fell far behind. For most Japanese women modern life during the interwar years remained an ideal rather than reality. Remarkably, a 1920 photograph of members of the feminist Bluestocking Society (*Seitō*) shows all militant ladies clad in kimono.[14]

However, modernity should not merely be defined as Western. Although women's kimono of the period mainly showed traditional designs, after the earthquake the new type of *meisen* kimono became popular. In contrast to traditional kimono, *meisen* kimono were sold ready-made by department stores (fig. 15). Since they were much cheaper than the traditional ones, the new garments lasted often no longer than a single season. Thereby kimono fashion accelerated its pace. Especially popular were geometrical designs reminiscent of Art Deco, which introduced a new kind of aesthetics to kimono fashion.

10. Hand-bill (*hikifusa*) of the Sumida kimono shop in Kobe (1910). Such lithograph prints with advertisements were distributed among the best customers. Author's collection

Women's kimono at the upper end of the market were mainly decorated with medium-large traditional designs in vibrant colours: in particular, flowers, birds (alone or in combination [*kachō*]), and views of famous places (*meisho*). The designs, always worn in harmony with the season, often demonstrated the much admired ability that Japanese artists have for 'intimate observation of nature'. Such luxury items were still decorated by hand in a variety of techniques.

In contrast, most urban men dressed in Western-style suits with Maurice Chevalier straw hats, and later felt hats, but at home they changed to the comfortable cotton *yukata* kimono. Men with a more traditional inclination wore plain dark kimono in combination with a jacket and an under-kimono. The latter two had concealed designs that reflected the wearer's personal interests in traditional culture, such as kabuki, *nō*-theatre and the tea ceremony, or contemporary pastimes like baseball, horse racing and politics.

Department stores continued to commission from well-known artists designs for advertisements with beautiful women dressed in trendy kimono. Extant examples are known by Itō Shinsui (1898–1972), Kitano Tsunetomi (1880–1947) (fig. 16), Sugiura Hisui (1876–1965) and Nakamura Daizaburō (1898–1947).[15] Similarly, painters benefited from the skills of kimono designers: several specialists in the revived genre of *bijinga* (pictures of beautiful women) took lessons from kimono designers to familiarise themselves with the representation of kimono patterns on their prints or paintings.[16]

What is considered 'Taishō Culture', and had started right after the Great War, in fact spilled over into the beginning of the reign of Emperor Hirohito and lasted until 1937. These years were certainly no less hectic than the reign of Hirohito's father had been.

The 1929 World Depression struck Japan with great force, especially in the silk-producing areas on the countryside where the loss of demand from the American market was bitterly felt. The collapse of world trade due to the tariff barriers of protectionism isolated and damaged Japan because the country lacked raw materials. In certain circles of the military a longing arose to create an autarky, an empire that would be independent from the whims of international trade. Manchuria, with its ore-rich soil and already dominated by Japan through the Kwantung army and the South Manchurian Railways, offered a luring perspective. The 1931–33 Manchurian Incident brought indeed the complete Japanese control over all of north-eastern China, but further aggravated Japan's isolation and led to its withdrawal from the League of Nations.

From the early 1930s onward, the Shōwa era ('Illustrious Peace') was characterised by rising militarism and hostilities to China, culminating in the outbreak of the disastrous China War (1937–45). It was not rare for war motifs to appear on children's and men's kimono.[17]

11. Page from a woodblock-printed kimono design book (*hinagatabon*). Author's collection

THE GREAT EARTHQUAKE AND FIRE OF TOKYO.

大正12.9.1 東京大震災 上野廣小路附近震災後の惨状

THE MATSUZAKAYA DEPARTMENT STORE AT UENO, TOKYO. 上野廣小路松坂屋百貨店の壯観 （東京名所）

Ginza Dori, Tokyo. 銀座通

16. Poster designed for Takashimaya by Kitano Tsunetomi in 1916. Takashimaya Historical Museum, Osaka

17. Postcard of a Ginza sidewalk *ca.* 1937. Courtesy of Steve Sundberg, OldTokyo.com

18. Wartime working woman in baggy trousers (*mompe*). Postcard, author's collection

Despite the growing isolation of the country and rising nationalism, Western dress among women gained some ground. A 1937 nationwide survey among 26,000 women found that 13% of women in Tokyo and 12% of women in Osaka wore Western dress. In the central Marunouchi area of Tokyo 39% of professional working women wore Western dress (fig. 17).[18] Nevertheless, even in urban areas, the large majority of women dressed traditionally. During World War II clothing materials became scarce. According to the Ministry of Culture and Industry, women between 20 and 40 years of age owned an average of forty dresses, double the number owned by women in America, 'the home of decadence'.[19] These figures indicate how prosperous the Taishō and early Shōwa periods had been despite a series of ups and downs. For the Minister they were merely proof of extravagance and waste: "One bolt of cloth [per woman] – that meant 500 airplanes or 5390 tanks that we can't send to the battlefront". From 1942 clothing and fabrics were rationed by a points system. Standard men's and women's attire were designed in the national defence colour, khaki. Working women were required to wear baggy *mompe* trousers made of indigo cotton (fig. 18). Where cotton was not available, silk kimono were cut up to make working clothes.

After the war, poverty and the overwhelming influx of American culture prevented an early recovery of kimono manufacture on a large scale. It was only after the spectacular reconstruction of the country during the 1950s that Japan's national dress for women experienced a new and possibly last revival. Men did not join in.

[1] Chamberlain 1971.
[2] Dalby 2001: 66-67.
[3] Chamberlain 1971: 125.
[4] Rein 1889: 533-34, 544-47.
[5] Milhaupt 2006: 34-41.
[6] *Ibid.*: 37.
[7] Sapin 2004: 317-36.
[8] Brown 2004: 47-67.
[9] Clark 2000: 25-49.
[10] Tipton 2000: 119-37.
[11] Sand 2000: 99-118.
[12] Tipton 2005: 38-43.
[13] Sato 2003: 49.
[14] Tipton 2005: 40 (fig. 45).
[15] Milhaupt 2006.
[16] Van Assche 2005: 27.
[17] Atkins 2005.
[18] Sato 2004: 182, n. 4.
[19] Wakakuwa 2005.

Taishō Kimono
Structure, Fabric and Decoration

The word kimono – which means simply 'thing to wear' – was only introduced as a generic term for Japanese dress in the third quarter of the nineteenth century. In Tokugawa Japan, a great variety of words had existed for the different garments of people of different class, gender, age, profession, wealth, and for various occasions. After the Meiji Restoration, foreigners called all long tubular Japanese garments kimono, whereas the Japanese continued to use the specialised names most of the time. The word kimono only came to be commonly used in Japan as an alternative word for native dress (*wafuku*), as opposed to from Western dress (*yōfuku*).

A primary differentiation was made between formal/ceremonial dress (*haregi*) (fig. 19) and informal/everyday dress (*fudangi*); this distinction will be applied in the women's kimono section of this book.[1]

The structure

The structure of the kimono was rather simple. The average lady's kimono was typically made out of a single bolt of fabric, roughly 10-12 metres long and 30-40 centimetres wide (fig. 20). The body consisted of two long panels, and the sleeves of two short panels, which were sewn into a whole without shoulder seams. As a consequence, if the kimono was cut from a bolt with repeating motifs, these motifs appeared upright on the back, but upside-down on the front. The remainder of the bolt was used to extend the front panels breadthways, and to cut the lapels and the collar. The extended front panels enabled front wrapping: left over right (only after death: right over left). The robe was held in place by a sash or *obi*. The construction was basically the same for men's and women's kimono, but for small chil-

19. Couple in ceremonial dress on the occasion of the 50th anniversary of a relative's wedding. Both are wearing an outfit with five crests: the gentleman in black *habutae* silk jacket, kimono and split trousers (*hakama*), the lady in black kimono (*kurotomesode*) with *yūzen* design. Ikjeld.com

20a. Bolt of silk measuring about 10-12 metres by 30-40 centimetres from which the various parts for the kimono were cut: B – body, S – sleeve, N – neckband and collar, O – overlap
20b. Basic structure of the kimono: B – body, S – sleeve, N – neckband and collar, O – overlap

21. Miniature kimono (*hinagata*) made of cotton, such as made by schoolgirls for practice (53 × 42 cm). Author's collection

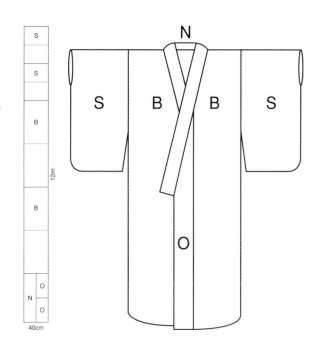

dren's kimono only single back panels and half-width front panels sufficed.

Although department stores and specialist dealers played the prominent roles in the trade and silk kimono were seldom manufactured at home, most girls learned the elements of kimono cutting at school. Such miniature kimono (*hinagata*) were normally made of inexpensive cotton (fig. 21). Despite its simple construction, the cleaning of a kimono was not easy. Should the garment be washed as a whole, the kimono would come out disfigured. Therefore the kimono needed to be taken apart before cleaning, and, after washing, the various panels were dried on wooden boards to retain their straight shapes. Finally the kimono was sewn into a whole garment again (fig. 22). The simple structure was in fact a continuation of the *kosode* ('small sleeves') from the Tokugawa period. This garment had smaller sleeve openings and the sleeves were completely attached to the body without openings at the armpits. The *kosode* in its turn derived from the inner layers of the exuberant twelve-layers robe (*jūni-hitoe*) worn by court ladies in the Heian era (794–1185). Like so many things in Japan, this undergarment had evolved from a Chinese model: the *tarikubi*, a robe worn at court in China during the Tang Dynasty (618–907).

Since very little cutting was done, the surfaces of the front, the back and even of the sleeves were flat and therefore invited decorations. Differences in taste, wealth, education, and marital status were revealed by the decoration of the kimono and the kind of fabric from which it was made.

The fabric

The great majority of professionally manufactured kimono were made of silk. Although the decoration generally remained executed by hand at the beginning of the twentieth century, the silks were usually machine-woven. Common types of silk were *habutae*, *chirimen*, *kinsha,* and *ro* (fig. 23).

– *Habutae* is a smooth and glossy plain weave that resembles taffeta. This black fabric was the standard material for men's undecorated formal garments (fig. 23a).

– *Chirimen* or crepe silk was produced with a distinctive technique in which the weft threads were twisted or 'overspun'. This provided the fabric with a fine drape and a pleasant texture (fig. 23b).

– *Kinsha* or fine crepe was produced in a similar way to *chirimen*, but with a lesser degree of twist in the weft threads. Both kinds of crepe were commonly used for women's and girls' kimono (fig. 23c).

– *Ro* or gauze weave shows strips of densely woven plain weave separated by open weave. Such open weave fabrics were favoured in summertime (fig. 23d).

For working class people and in rural areas cotton was the standard fabric for kimono, often dyed with natural or chemical indigo. Occasionally other fabrics were used. Hemp cloth (*asa*)

22. To be washed, kimono had to be taken apart. The panels were subsequently dried on wooden boards to prevent disfiguration.
Postcard, author's collection

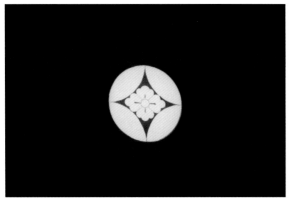
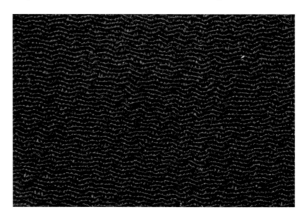
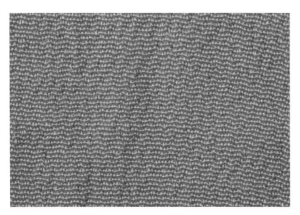

23. Magnifications of four common types of silk fabrics used for kimono: (a) *habutae*, (b) *chirimen*, (c) *kinsha*, (d) *ro*

24. Lithograph in the shape of a fan showing a young woman selecting a bolt of silk; over the stand a loosely sewn *karinui* is displayed (1903). Author's collection

25. Hand-painted images of Daruma on the lining of a man's jacket by Suzuki Shōnen (1849–1918). The ink has eaten through the silk. Collection Eric van den Ing (Netherlands)

was pleasant to wear in summer, and during the 1920s rayon was introduced. *Yukata*, simple cotton kimono worn in and around the house, were always made of cotton.

Kimono linings were made from cheaper kinds of silk or even from cotton or rayon.

The decoration

The decoration required careful planning, since the design nearly always continued over more than one panel. Very often, the decoration was done before the garment was sewn into a whole. Kimono were generally offered for sale either as bolts or as *karinui* (fig. 24). *Karinui* were display-kimono, of which the panels had been temporarily sewn with basting stitches into a whole garment to enable judgement of the complete design. Adjustments to the customer's measures could therefore still be easily carried out.

The choice of refined or daring designs was especially important for geisha as they were professional kimono wearers. Designs of this nature were very often made to order. In her memoirs, Iwasaki Mineko, the leading geisha of Kyoto's Gion quarter in the 1970s, recalls:

"Kimono were my passion and I took an active role in their design and conception. My greatest pleasure was to meet the venerable Mr Iida at Takashimaya, or Mr Saito at Gofukiya, or the skilled staff of Eriman and Ichizo, to talk about my ideas for new patterns and colour combinations."[2]

She estimated that she had owned more than 300 kimono during her career, each costing between £ 3,000 and £ 5,000 – the most special pieces not included.

It was not at all exceptional for the design to be chosen by the customer from plates in painted or printed design sample books (*hinagatabon*), which could then be adapted to the personal wishes of the client.

Hinagatabon have been published since the seventeenth century. Examples of kimono design drawings are known by famous painters like Hishikawa Morunobu (1618–94), Maruyama Ōkyo (1733–95), Kishi Chikudō (1826–97), Imao Keinen (1845–1924), Nakamura Daizaburō (1898–1947), Takeuchi Seihō (1864–1942), and Kamisaka Sekka (1866–1942).[3] There also existed a tradition of direct painting on kimono by professional painters. Surviving examples were painted by Ogata Kōrin (1658–1716), Matsumura Goshun (1752–1811), Sakai Hōitsu (1761–1828) and Suzuki Shōnen (1849–1918) (fig. 25).[4] However, it is extremely rare to come across such items. In general, the influences by the great artists were indirect. Also most *hinagatabon* were not made by famous painters but by local artists in connection with merchants for

27. Ceremonial man's jacket with five crests (cat. 43)

28. Three versions of the crests in decreasing order of formality: (a) recto crest (*omote mon*), (b) verso crest (*ura mon*), (c) embroidered crest (*nui mon*)

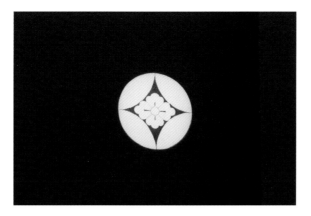

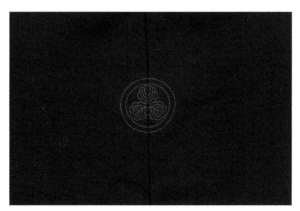

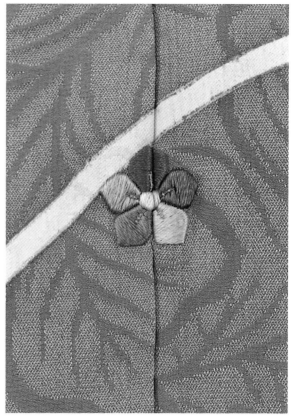

whom they worked (figs. 11, 26). These merchants played a key role in the production process by coordinating the design drawing, dyeing and weaving.

The various decoration techniques will be explained in the introductions to the chapters in which textiles with these techniques are most frequently shown: *yūzen* in formal women's kimono, *meisen* in women's informal kimono, *rinzu* in women's jackets, *kata-yūzen* in men's jackets and under-kimono, *nishiki* in sashes and men's jackets, *tegaki-yūzen* and *nui* in children's kimono, whereas in the entries of several individual textiles *shibori* (cat. 8, 91), *kasuri* (cat. 99) and *tsume tsuzure* (cat. 111) will be discussed.

Among other things, such as the kind of fabric used and the sort of design employed, the number of crests (one, three or five) on a kimono or *haori* decided the degree of formality: one at the top centre of the back, three with additional crests on the back of the sleeves, or five with two extra crests at the top of the front panels (fig. 27). The absence of crests meant informal dress, five crests meant ceremonial dress. When kimono were shown in shops or department stores in their temporary shapes of *karinui*, the places for the crests were left blank.

Crests came in different versions (fig. 28). The official recto version (*omote mon*) appeared as a white symbol against a black background (fig. 28a). The verso crest (*ura mon*) only showed the

white outline of the symbol and was considered less formal (fig. 28b), whereas the embroidered crest (*nui mon*) could even be merely decorative (fig. 28c).

Although the wearing of crests was strictly regulated during the early Tokugawa period, at the beginning of the twentieth century every Japanese family was entitled to use crests, but their history may have been very short. Sometimes families used two crests, one for ceremonial occasions and the other for less formal gatherings. Married women occasionally preferred to wear their maiden's crest. In general the heraldic significance of crests was much less than it had been in feudal times.[5]

[1] Dalby 2001: 171-84.
[2] Iwasaki & Brown 2003: 264.
[3] *Kamisaka Sekka: Rimpa Master* (exh. cat.) 2003: 134, 249.
[4] Watson 1981: 222 (*kosode* painted by Sakai Hōitsu).
[5] Dower 2005.

Women's Formal and Ceremonial Kimono
A Celebration of Tradition

Women's formal and ceremonial dress (*haregi*) comprised a range of kimono varieties: *furisode*, *uchikake*, *kurotomesode*, *irotomesode*, *hōmongi* and *tsukesage*. Women took great care to make the appropriate choice of which kimono to wear on special occasions.

Unquestionably, the *furisode* with its very long, fluttering sleeves was the most elegant of these robes (cat. 1–8). *Furisode* means 'swinging sleeves'. In fact, the sleeves were not longer than the ones of any other type of kimono (the length from shoulder to underarm is the same), but they were extremely wide, often reaching to the ankles. *Furisode* were exclusively worn by unmarried young women: the younger the woman, the longer the sleeves. The seams of the sleeves were mostly rounded, like those of children's kimono. Striking decorations, often in bright colours, covered most of their surfaces (fig. 29).

Uchikake or bridal kimono were worn loosely over other kimono (cat. 9–11). They were not front-wrapped and therefore a sash (*obi*) was superfluous. Like *furisode*, *uchikake* had long sleeves and all-over opulent decorations, often with symbols of good fortune or happiness for the occasion.

Married women dressed in kimono with smaller sleeves and less abundant decoration. Their ceremonial dress was the black *kurotomesode* (*kuro* means black, *tomesode* means 'truncated sleeve') with a decoration concentrated on the lower part, especially on the most exposed left front (cat. 12–15). Bold decorations extending up to the waist were meant for young married women, elderly ladies mostly wore *kurotomesode* with a design limited to the left front hem.

Irotomesode (*iro* means colour) were considered semi-full dress (cat. 16). The decoration against a coloured background was often applied on both front panels and overlaps with limited extension to the back. When these designs were identical, it was called *ryozuma* or mirror image – a style that was popular in the 1920s and 1930s.

Hōmongi or visiting wear was also considered semi-full dress and adorned with extensive asymmetrical decorations (cat. 17). The related *tsukesage*, which was

one step lower in the kimono hierarchy, featured a combined hem and shoulder decoration, leaving ample empty space at the waist for the wide *obi* (cat. 18). The *susohiki* ('trail the skirt') was much longer than all other types and worn exclusively by geisha for dancing (cat. 19): during the dance, the long hem would trail on the floor. During the Tokugawa period all kimono had been longer. Aristocratic ladies, but also high-class prostitutes, used to wear padded, trailing hems (*hikisuso*), however, in the early twentieth century any excess length was tucked away into a horizontal fold below the sash (fig. 7).

Unlike today, Taishō kimono were worn with an undergarment or *nagajuban* (cat. 11b, 20, 21). Most common were the bright red under-kimono with patterns in tie-dye (*shibori*), but also monochrome damask-weave silk (*rinzu*) and designs consisting of pattern samples were popular. The latter were derived from patchwork (*kiribame*) examples of the past. Sometimes the kimono and *nagajuban* formed a matching pair, and even sets of three kimono existed: a black outer kimono, a red middle kimono and a white under-kimono (cat. 7). In general, women's dress of the Taishō and early Shōwa periods had two or three layers and was worn more loosely than nowadays.

Formal and ceremonial kimono were always made of glossy, smooth silk. Cotton, wool and fibre fabrics were considered inappropriate for that purpose, and so was non-glossy raw silk. Decorations were always dyed (*somemono*). Woven patterns (*orimono*) were unsuitable for ceremonial wear, except the subtle *ton-sur-ton* figured silk or damask weave (*rinzu*), which was regularly used as a background.

The subject matter of formal or ceremonial kimono was traditional if not nostalgic. After the wave of Westernisation in the early Meiji period, the beginning of the twentieth century experienced a renewed interest in traditional subjects and motifs. In addition, the kimono had become recognised as Japan's national costume. Therefore it is no wonder that, especially during traditional festive occasions like coming of age ceremonies or weddings, Japanese dress with subjects reminiscent of the past were favoured (fig. 30). Floral

29. Group of apprentice geisha (*maiko*) in *furisode* sitting on the veranda. Postcard, author's collection

30. Photograph of the parental family of Princess Nagako, the future empress (early 1920s). The three young ladies are dressed in long-sleeved *furisode*, the mother in *kurotomesode*, all with traditional designs

motifs such as chrysanthemums, peonies, plum, bamboo, pine trees and flower balls were frequently depicted. Among the animal subjects, birds were the most popular subjects: the *hōō* for bridal kimono, but above anything else the crane. The crane itself had become a symbol of Japan. Little children also appeared on ladies' kimono, as did famous scenic spots, decorated fans, butterflies, etc. Remarkably popular were motifs from the Heian era (795–1185), such as court ladies, ox carriages and the boxes of the shell game (*kaoike*). Department stores had considerable influence on fashion. Using geisha as models, a revival of Genroku style (1688–1704) kimono with greatly enlarged designs was successfully promoted from 1906 onwards. Examples of this fashion in the present collection are the *furisode* with gigantic snow crystals and the *furisode* with enormous pine branches (cat. 1, 2). Of course, the chosen design had to be appropriate for the occasion and season.

A variety of decoration techniques can be observed, such as tie-dye (*shibori*), brocade weaving (*nishiki*) and embroidery (*nui*), but the prime technique in Taishō ceremonial and formal dress for women was *yūzen*. Actually, the first half of the twentieth century was one of the flourishing periods of the *yūzen* technique. It had a long history. Already during the seventeenth century, painters were asked to decorate *kosode* for the wives and daughters of wealthy merchants. However, such decorations were not very durable and poorly resistant to washing. The Kyoto fan painter Miyazaki Yūzen is credited for the invention in 1687 of a new, more durable painterly technique of decorating *kosode*. The word *yūzen* usually refers to the *tsutsugaki-yūzen*

technique. After drawing a fine outline of the design on the silk fabric with a fluid made from the *Commelina communis* plant, the outlines were covered with glutinous rice paste by making use of a bag with a very thin spout (like those used for cake decoration). The entire cloth was then covered with soy bean milk to prevent blurring of the dyes. Subsequently, the spaces within the outlines were painted with a brush in various colours, whereby the rice paste prevented the dyes from spreading. The total design was then covered with rice paste-resist to enable brushing the background into the desired colour (for example, black for a *kurotomesode*). The last steps were steaming to fix the colours and rinsing in running water to remove the rice paste and tracing fluid. The result was a decoration in bright colours surrounded by thin white lines (fig. 31). The most elaborate *yūzen* kimono were enlivened with embroidery and the application of gold thread or gold leaf on the white outlines.

The term *yūzen* is sometimes confusing, since it comprises several other techniques apart from *tsutsugaki-yūzen*. The essence is that *yūzen* implies painting with a washable fixative to keep the dyes in place and prevent them from later bleeding. Two variants will be discussed in other chapters: freehand painting (*tegaki-yūzen*) and direct-dye stencil-printing (*kata-yūzen*).

Kyoto has always been the main centre for *yūzen* work (*Kyō yūzen*), but Kanazawa – the city where Miyazaki Yūzen moved to later – was also famous for silk decoration in this technique (*Kaga yūzen*), and to a lesser degree Tokyo (*Edo yūzen*) and Nagoya (*Nagoya yūzen*) as well.

1. Genroku-style

Woman's *furisode* (three crests)
Outside: off-white crepe silk (*chirimen*);
hand-painted with rice-paste resist
outlining (*yūzen*), embroidery, extensive
couching of gold thread and extensive
application of gold and silver leaf
Crest: chrysanthemum (*kiku*)
Lining: red silk
166 × 130 cm
1905–20

Five enormous overlapping snow-crystal
roundels (*yukiwa*) and two giant
folding fans form the basic pictorial
elements of this opulent kimono.
Sweeping bamboo, floral roundels
and flower balls with their long cords
traverse these basic elements, so
creating a very dynamic design.
Such bold design elements – popular
during the Taishō period – were
elaborations of examples from the
Genroku era (1688–1704).
The ostentatious design not only
continues from back to front, but
also from the back onto the sleeves.
Numerous flowers and trailing cords
have been finely embroidered, small
motifs on extensive areas have been
applied in gold or silver foil. The edges
of the ribs of the folding fans and the
edges of the bamboo leaves are couched
with gold thread.

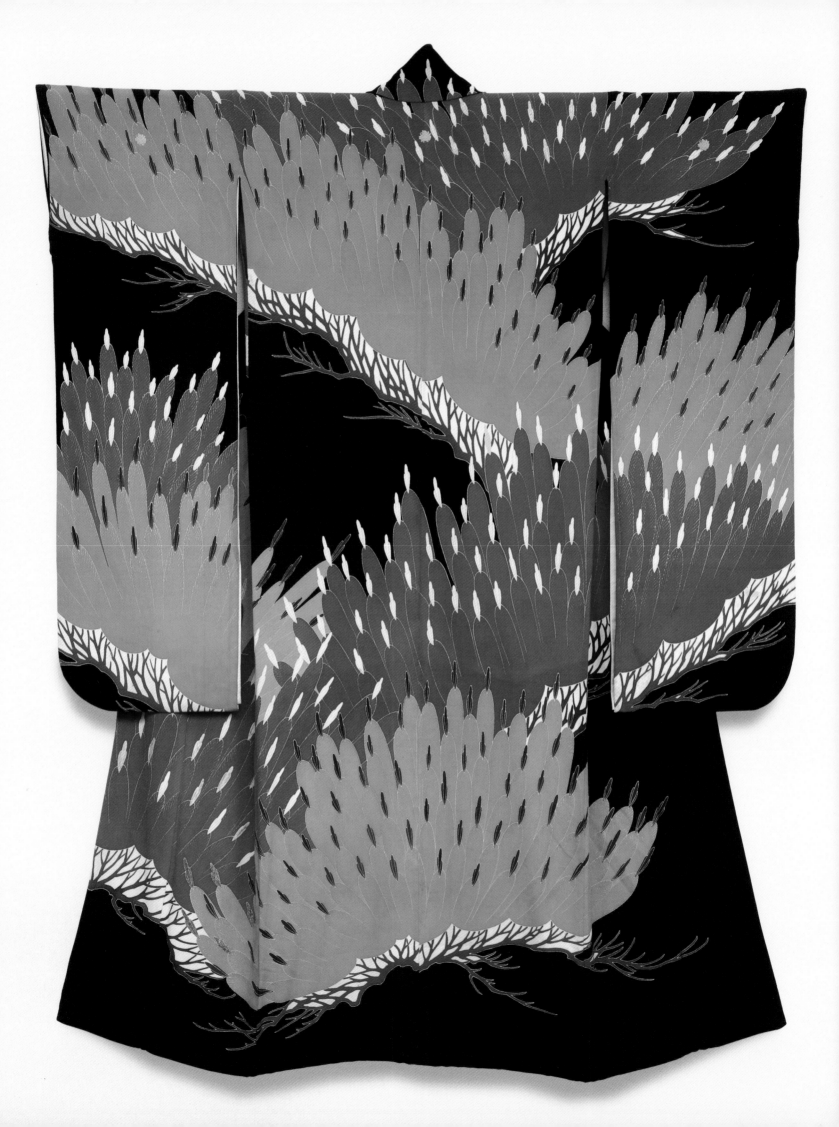

2. Pine branches

Woman's *furisode* (five crests)
Outside: black crepe silk (*chirimen*);
hand-painted with rice-paste resist
outlining (*yūzen*), embroidery
and application of gold foil
Crest: butterfly (*chō*)
Lining: red and white silk; lightly
padded
168 × 131 cm
1905–20

Eye-catching yellow and red pine
branches cover most of the surface
of this black 'swinging sleeves' kimono
for a young unmarried lady. Gold foil
details have been applied on the
bunches of needles, some of their tips
are embroidered. The sleeves are more
than one metre long.

3. A myriad of flying cranes
Woman's *furisode* (one crest)
Outside; black crepe silk (*chirimen*);
hand-painted with rice-paste resist
outlining (*yūzen*) and application
of gold foil
Crest: bamboo (*take*)
Lining: red silk
158 × 127 cm
1910–30

Dozens of cranes are flying upwards.
Most birds are white, some red.
In the direction of the shoulders
the cranes become smaller in size.
Their outlines are often accentuated
with glittering gold foil, even on the
inside of the left front bottom, an area
that is sometimes exposed during
walking. The total number of birds
is over two hundred.
In Japan the crane is held in high
esteem, and regarded as an emblem
of long life and happiness.

4. Cranes flying above pine trees

Woman's *furisode* (three crests)
Outside: black crepe silk (*chirimen*);
hand-painted with rice-paste resist
outlining (*yūzen*) and embroidery
Crest: arrow feathers (*yabane*)
Lining: red silk
152 × 122 cm
1920–40

High above the pine trees, white cranes
with black tails are circling in the air.
Their crowns are done in red *sagara-nui*
(French knot) embroidery, their eyes in
black and yellow embroidery, and their
necks in white embroidery. The pines
have been painted directly without
paste-resist outlining. The needles
within the green areas were left blank,
which creates an impressionistic
atmosphere that is further enhanced
by the graded 'light' between the trees.
Red silk linings are a characteristic
of Taishō kimono. At the sleeves they
appear as red edges, contrasting with
the black outside. After World War II
red linings fell out of fashion.

5. New Year

Woman's *furisode* (five crests)
Outside: white silk; damask weave
(*rinzu*) with freehand painting
(*tegaki-yūzen*)
Crest: mesh (*meyui*)
Lining: white silk; lightly padded hem
163 × 130 cm
1920–40

On the background of a wattle fence in
damask weave, bamboo, plum, berries,
pine and vine have been painted vividly.
The large bamboo stalk on the right
lapel has clearly been created by the
freehand stroke of a large brush
(*tegaki-yūzen*).
Such an elegant, but formal, *furisode*
with a combination of plants on
a snow-white ground may have been
worn by a young unmarried woman
on the occasion of New Year, plum
being the first tree to blossom each
year. It was fashionable to wear designs
slightly ahead of the season.

6. Majestic white *hōō*
Woman's *furisode* (five crests)
Outside: old rose crepe silk (*chirimen*);
hand-painted with rice-paste resist
outlining (*yūzen*) and gold foil
application
Crest: paulownia (*kiri*)
Lining: red silk
158 × 130 cm
1920–40

This *furisode* shows a majestic *hōō*-bird
in various shades of white with accents
in red, orange, ivory and green;
the ends of the tail feathers are dyed
turquoise, blue and red like those of
peacocks. The chrysanthemums and
paulownias on the sleeves are rendered
in a painterly way. The combination
of motifs is associated with the imperial
family. On the insides of the lower
front, colourful bamboo leaves have
been added.
One wonders whether the combination
of the paulownia crest with the large
paulownia motifs on the right sleeve
means that the *furisode* was made
to order.

7. Cranes flying above the sea
Set of three woman's *furisode*
(five crests)

7a. Woman's *furisode* with lightly padded hem (five crests)
Outside: black fine crepe silk (*kinsha*);
hand-painted with rice-paste resist
outlining (*yūzen*), gold foil application,
embroidery and splashing (*nori-koboshi*)
Crest: wild carnation (*nadeshiko*)
Lining: red silk
163 × 124 cm
1920–40

This is the outer garment from a set
of three *furisode* in the classical colour
sequence: black, red and white.
The contrasting colours were only
visible at the ends of the sleeves, at the
neck, and perhaps a little at the hem.
The patterns of flying cranes above the
boisterous sea are similar, but the outer
furisode is decorated most lavishly with
additional mountains and islands grown
with pines, blooming plums and
bamboo. On some of the hills buildings
are depicted.
The *yūzen*-work is of exceptional
quality, and so is the very fine French
knot embroidery on the heads of the
cranes (*sagara-nui*) and the flat-stitch
embroidery (*hira-nui*) on the wings
of the birds, the plum blossoms and
the crests of the waves. The boisterous
character of the waves is increased by
white splashes of paint (*nori-koboshi*)
that has been blown onto the textile.
In order to enhance the glittering effect
even more, random stitches of silver
thread have been applied. Note the fine
grading (*bokashi*) of the background
from black to blue and white.

7b. Woman's *furisode* (five crests),
part of a set
Outside: red fine crepe silk (*kinsha*);
hand-painted with rice-paste resist
outlining (*yūzen*), gold foil application,
embroidery and splashing (*nori-koboshi*)
Crest: wild carnation (*nadeshiko*)
Lining: red silk
163 × 124 cm
1920–40

Layered sets are called *o-tsui*, the outer
garment *uwagi* and the underlayers
shitagi.
The second layer, which is the first
shitagi, has a simpler decoration
and less embroidery than the *uwagi*.
Above the waves, bands of gold foil
suggest haze.

7c. Woman's *furisode* (five crests),
part of a set
Outside: white fine crepe silk (*kinsha*);
hand-painted with rice-paste resist
outlining (*yūzen*), gold foil application,
embroidery and splashing (*nori-koboshi*)
Crest: wild carnation (*nadeshiko*)
Lining: red silk
161 × 124 cm
1920–40

The innermost white layer, the second
shitagi, is always the dirtiest and most
damaged, consequently, sets of three
kimono in good condition are rare.
Nowadays, the kimono tradition has
become more uniform and simple
and such sets are no longer worn.
Only the crests of the cranes and their
eyes are embroidered. Like on the other
pieces of this set, also the front shows
several flying cranes around the collar.
Whereas the outer layers have white
nadeshiko crests, on the white *furisode*
these are applied in gold foil.

8. Peonies

Woman's *furisode* (no crests)
Outside: marine silk; plain weave with tie-dye (*shibori*) decoration
Inside: white silk with orange borders; damask weave
161 × 124 cm
1960–80

Thousands of tie-dyed dots within squares (*hon hitta kanoko*) form the background for the large peonies and their leaves. The relief of such all-over *shibori* kimono with decorations in reverse image gives these textiles a characteristic texture.

Before being immersed in the dye bath, each of the countless dots had been attached to a sharp hook on a short vertical pole and wound several times round with a thin thread. In doing so the surface of the textile became much smaller because of the numerous raised tufts of silk. After the dye bath, the dyer would strongly pull the piece of textile in several directions, thereby breaking all the wound threads.

The end result is a textured silk decorated with white circles or squares (see detail).

Since the beginning of the Tokugawa period, the village of Arimatsu on the Tōkaidō road between Osaka and Edo (now Tokyo) has been the centre of *shibori* production. After World War II a last flourishing period was the result of successful export to Africa. Although this *furisode* dates from around 1970, the bold design could equally have featured on a garment of the Taishō period (see illustration). Styles were rarely abandoned in Japan.

Detail of the tie-dye technique

Woodblock print *Tsume* or 'nails' by Itō Shinsui (1898–1972), published by Watanabe Shōzaburō in 1936, Wiebrens collection (Netherlands). Painters and print designers of the early twentieth century often depicted the kimono of their beautiful women in great detail, such as this *shibori* gown

9. Brocade chrysanthemums

Woman's padded *uchikake* (no crests)
Outside: beige silk, brocade weave
(*nishiki*)
Lining: red silk
168 × 125 cm
1900–20

This bridal kimono in subdued colours
and medium-long sleeves probably
dates from late Meiji (1869–1912) or
early Taishō (1912–26). The decoration
consists of a multitude of
chrysanthemums. Together with the
cherry, the chrysanthemum is the most
admired flower in Japan; a stylised
representation of a chrysanthemum
with sixteen petals forms the crest
of the imperial family.
The weaving has been carried out with
fine detailing of flowers and leaves.
For contrast, the bright red lining
sticks out slightly from the sleeves
and is more pronounced at the thickly
padded hem.
During the Tokugawa period
(1600–1868), *uchikake* had been worn
as cloaks over the *kosode* by ladies
of the ruling class.

10. 'Three friends'
Woman's padded *uchikake* (no crests)
Outside: beige silk, brocade weave
(*nishiki*)
Lining: red silk decorated in
block-clamp-resist dyeing (*itajime*)
168 × 127 cm
1910–20

The gold impression in this bridal
kimono is given by the abundant gold
clouds and bamboo stalks, which are
woven into the beige silk. Both gold-
enfolded threads and thin gold paper
strips have been used. Interestingly the
gold-woven bamboo stalks feature the
square patterns as if they were done
in the tie-dye *shibori* technique.
Against this 'golden' background a
colourful decoration has been woven in
two kinds of blue, two kinds of green,
two kinds of brown, two kinds of gold,
off-white and purple. The bright red
lining is done in the block clamp-resist
dyeing technique (*itajime*), which was
popular during the Meiji era.
The motifs of bamboo leaves, pine trees
and flowering plum form together the
so-called 'three friends' (*shōchikubai*),
a favourite subject in Japanese art with
Confucian connotations of loyalty.
Plum symbolises the rejuvenation of
beauty, bamboo is the strong plant that
bends to weather storms, and pine
is the emblem of evergreen old age.

**11. *Hōō*-bird, paulownia
and chrysanthemums**
Set of woman's *uchikake*
and *nagajuban*

11a. Woman's *uchikake*, padded
at the hem (three crests)
Outside: white silk; plain weave
with freehand painting (*tegaki-yūzen*)
and gold couching

Crest: bamboo (*take*)
Lining: red silk
156 × 122 cm
1920–40

The mythical *hōō*-bird – often
misleadingly called a phoenix – is
considered the most important of all
feathered creatures. Like on this
uchikake, the bird has feathers of five

colours, symbolising the cardinal
virtues: compassion, decency, wisdom,
faithfulness and gentleness. Its song
is lovely and said to consist of a
modulation on six notes.
In combination with the *Paulownia
imperialis*, the *hōō* symbolises imperial
power; on bridal kimono it refers to the
bride as an empress for one day.
Furthermore, the bird is an omen

of good luck and longevity, and an
emblem of connubial felicity as well.
Freehand brushstrokes can be clearly
recognised on this robe.
The white silk of the outside is so thin
that the bright red lining shines
through, thus creating a 'cherry
blossom' muted pink – an effect already
popular in the multi-layered gowns
of the Heian period (794–1185).

11b. Woman's padded *nagajuban* (five crests), part of the *uchikake* set
Outside: red crepe silk (*chirimen*); damask weave (*rinzu*) with gold couching
Crest: bamboo (*take*)
Lining: red crepe silk (*chirimen*); damask weave (*rinzu*)
149 × 122 cm
1920–40

In damask weave, this under-kimono of the *uchikake* shows large chrysanthemum flowers all over. The five crests have been created by securing double gold-enfolded threads with tiny red stitches.

12. A pair of pheasants in hiding
Woman's *kurotomesode* (five crests)
Outside: black silk, horizontal
gauze-weave silk (*ro*); hand-painted
with rice-paste resist outlining (*yūzen*)
and gold foil application
Crest: wood sorrel (*katabami*)
Unlined
170 × 129 cm
1920–40

This lightweight summer kimono made of sheer silk shows a multitude of flowers at the lower end. Among the tangle of leaves and flowers, lilies, wild carnations, maiden's flowers, Chinese bells, pampas grass, chrysanthemums and ivy can be recognised. On closer examination, one of the grasses appears to be the long tail feather of the male pheasant, hidden together with its female at the extreme left. The scanty colours and the black background suggest a moonlit night scene.

At first glance the autumnal subject seems to contradict the gauze-weave of a summer kimono. In traditional Japanese fashion, however, designs slightly anticipated the next season. Therefore this unlined kimono must have been worn during warm spells of weather in September or early October, and it expresses a longing for the approaching autumn.

13. The Itsukushima shrine

Woman's *kurotomesode* (five crests)
Outside: black fine crepe silk (*kinsha*);
hand-painted with rice-paste resist
outlining (*yūzen*) and embroidery
Crest: paulownia (*kiri*)
Lining: red silk
160 × 128 cm
1920–40

The Itsukushima shrine on the shore of Miyajima Island is classified as one of Japan's 'three best views'.
Erected in 1168, the shrine has been often immortalised in Japanese art throughout the ages. Originally, commoners were not allowed to set foot on this holy island, but had to approach the shrine by boat, entering through the flooded wooden *torii* in the bay. The present orange *torii* only dates from 1875.

The design has been executed in the classical rice-paste resist *yūzen* technique with the addition of embroidery in the pine trees, in the haze and in the hanging lanterns of the corridor.
Contrasting with the bird's eye view on the exterior, the inside of the left front shows an intimate spot with three stone lanterns under a pine tree.

14. Books

Woman's *kurotomesode* (five crests)
Outside: black fine crepe silk (*kinsha*);
hand-painted with rice-paste resist
outlining (*yūzen*) and gold foil
application
Crest: wood sorrel (*katabami*)
Lining: red silk
155 × 126 cm
1920–40

It seems that a book shelf has fallen
over, and that all the books are spread
over the floor. In between the books, a
golden diadem with attached white hair
can be discerned together with two
large chrysanthemums and a twig of
blooming cherry. Furthermore, there is
an open fan with a phoenix decoration.
The books have all kinds of
decorations: a stylised stream, plovers,
an old pine, bamboo, plum, etc.
On one of them a pine branch next to
a wooden corridor with a railing can be
recognised as the gallery (*hashigakari*)
to the *nō* stage. Are the books librettos
of *nō* plays? However, the opened books
do not show any texts, but merely
colourful designs. They might therefore
be textile pattern books (*hinagata bon*).

15. Musashibō Benkei

Woman's *kurotomesode* (five crests)
Outside: black fine crepe silk (*kinsha*);
hand-painted with rice-paste resist
outlining (*yūzen*) and gold foil
application
Crests: ivy (*tsuta*)
Lining: red silk
164 × 128 cm
1920–40

Having won the epic war against the
Taira in 1185, Yoshitsune unexpectedly
fell into disgrace with his elder brother,
the shogun Minamoto Yoritomo.
With a few faithful supporters he was
compelled to flee the capital Kyoto
to a supposed safe haven in the deep
north. The legendary wandering priest
Musashibō Benkei, a tall man with
a rough character, guided the group
through many precarious situations.
Kanjinchō is one of the most famous
kabuki plays that acts the drama out on
stage. The features of the kabuki actor
on this *kurotomesode* point to
Matsumoto Kōshirō VII (1870–1949),
who played the role of Benkei in the
play *Kanjinchō* numerous times during
the 1930s. In 1935 he commissioned a
woodblock print of himself in this role
(see illustration) from Natori Shunsen
(1886–1960).
As here, mountain priests or *yamabushi*
can be recognised by their characteristic
dress (*suzukake*), i.e., the small
hexagonal cap, baggy trousers, a collar
with six coloured tufts, the crests
of the eight-spoke Wheel of Law. etc.
The typical attributes, such as the
conch-shell trumpet, the rosary and the
rectangular robe box are absent here.
This striking design depicts the fierce
priest in the frozen theatrical *mie* pose,
in which the character contemplates the
dramatic events. The bold inscription
in bright colours is a quotation from
an epic poem that describes Benkei's
pathetic circumstances. The text reads:

Wearing the *suzukake* as a travel
costume
I am immersed in sorrow, my sleeves
wet with dew

It is quite conceivable that such a
daring design was commissioned by
someone with connections in the world
of theatre, not necessarily a married
lady, but perhaps a geisha.

Woodblock print *The Subscription List*
by Natori Shunsen (1886–1960),
published by Watanabe Shōzaburō in
1935. Matsumoto Kōshirō VII in the
role of Benkei in the play *Kanjinchō*.
Arendie and Henk Herwig collection
(Netherlands)

16. Roosters and hens

Woman's *irotomesode* (five crests)
Outside: blue fine crepe silk (*kinsha*);
hand-painted with rice-paste resist
outlining (*yūzen*) and embroidery
Crest: wood sorrel (*katabami*)
Lining: red silk
159 × 126 cm
1920–40

Next to the black *kurotomesode*, the
coloured *irotomesode* is the second most
formal kimono for married women.
Irotomesode were worn on festive
occasions.
The back of this kimono is left
undecorated. The front shows roosters
and hens, both outside and inside.
The combs of the roosters and the
hearts of most chrysanthemums have
French knot embroidery (*sagara-nui*);
the eyes and nails of the fowl are
executed in flat embroidery. To some
of the green leaves a few stitches of gold
thread have been added to enhance
their reflection.

17. Fragrant flower balls
Woman's *hōmongi* (one crest)
Outside: cinnamon crepe
silk (*chirimen*), damask weave;
hand-painted with rice-paste resist
outlining (*yūzen*), embroidery
and gold thread couching
Crest: Chinese bell flower (*kikyō*)
Lining: red silk
147 × 126 cm
1920–40

Colourful flower balls with their long
cords dominate this *hōmongi* visiting
kimono. The decoration is mainly done
in the classical *yūzen* technique with
its white outlines, and the addition
of fine embroidery on some flowers.
The large Chinese bell flowers in two
of the four medallions are identical
to the embroidered flower of the family
crest, which might suggest that this
kimono was made to order.
However, embroidered crests (*nui mon*)
were considered less formal than dyed
crests, and may even have been merely
decorative elements.
The cinnamon coloured silk is figured
with leaves in damask weave.

18. Chrysanthemums

Woman's *tsukesage* (no crests)
Outside: red fine crepe silk (*kinsha*);
hand-painted with rice-paste resist
outlining (*yūzen*) and application
of gold foil.
Lining: cream and red silk
164 × 128 cm
1920–40

A *tsukesage* is a less formal kimono
(especially when crests are lacking)
with a vertically oriented design at the
hem, and with the same decorations
on the sleeves. The design will therefore
not be interrupted by the *obi*.
At first glance the groups of
chrysanthemums seem to repeat,
but in fact they are all different.

19. Tatsuta River
Geisha's *susohiki* (no crests)
Outside: black crepe silk (*chirimen*);
hand-painted with rice-paste resist
outlining (*yūzen*) and gold and silver
foil application
Lining: light grey silk lining
of the lower part of the body
202 × 127 cm
1920–40

This very long kimono was used
by a geisha as a dancing gown,
the excess length trailing on the floor.
The stylised water would
no doubt start flowing with her
movements.
The combination of waves and falling
or floating maple leaves points to
the Tatsuta River, a subject depicted

countless times in all fields of Japanese
art. It is also the title of a *nō* drama
by Zeami (1363–1408), in which the
red leaves on the water of the river
are compared with brocade.
The same metaphor had already been
used in an anonymous *tanka* poem
in the ancient anthology *Kokinshū*
(completed around the year 905):

A covering of
Bright scattered leaves floats on
Tatsuta River –
Were I to ford the waters
The brocade would tear in half

Translation by Laurel Lesplica Rodd
(Rodd & Henkenius 1996: 128)

20. Floral medallions

Woman's *nagajuban* (no crests)
Outside: red silk; damask weave (*rinzu*)
with tie-dye (*shibori*) decoration
Lining: red silk lining of the body
135 × 128 cm
1920–40

The damask woven fabric shows an
all-over key-fret pattern (*sayagata*) with
scattered floral ornaments. In *shibori*,
vertical undulating lines and cloud
patterns have been superimposed,
together with two large-size medallions
of chrysanthemums and hollyhocks.
Since the sleeves are long, this must
have been an under-kimono for
a *furisode*.

21. Pattern samples

Woman's *nagajuban* (no crests)
Outside: fine crepe silk (*kinsha*);
damask weave with stencil-printed,
direct-dye method decoration
(*kata-yūzen*) and gold foil additions;
attached collar in embroidery
Lining: plain weave cotton
134 × 120 cm
1920–40

This undergarment is decorated with eleven different textile patterns; their blue printed numbers have been left in place. It seems to be an autumn garment, since falling and floating leaves are the theme of several designs. All samples share a small flower motif woven into the fabric.

Although detachable collars (*han'eri*) are as a rule plain white nowadays, their precursors from the beginning of the twentieth century exhibit much more variety, such as this example in *ton-sur-ton* embroidery on crepe silk. Since kimono were not wrapped as tightly as today, a larger part of the *han'eri* was visible.

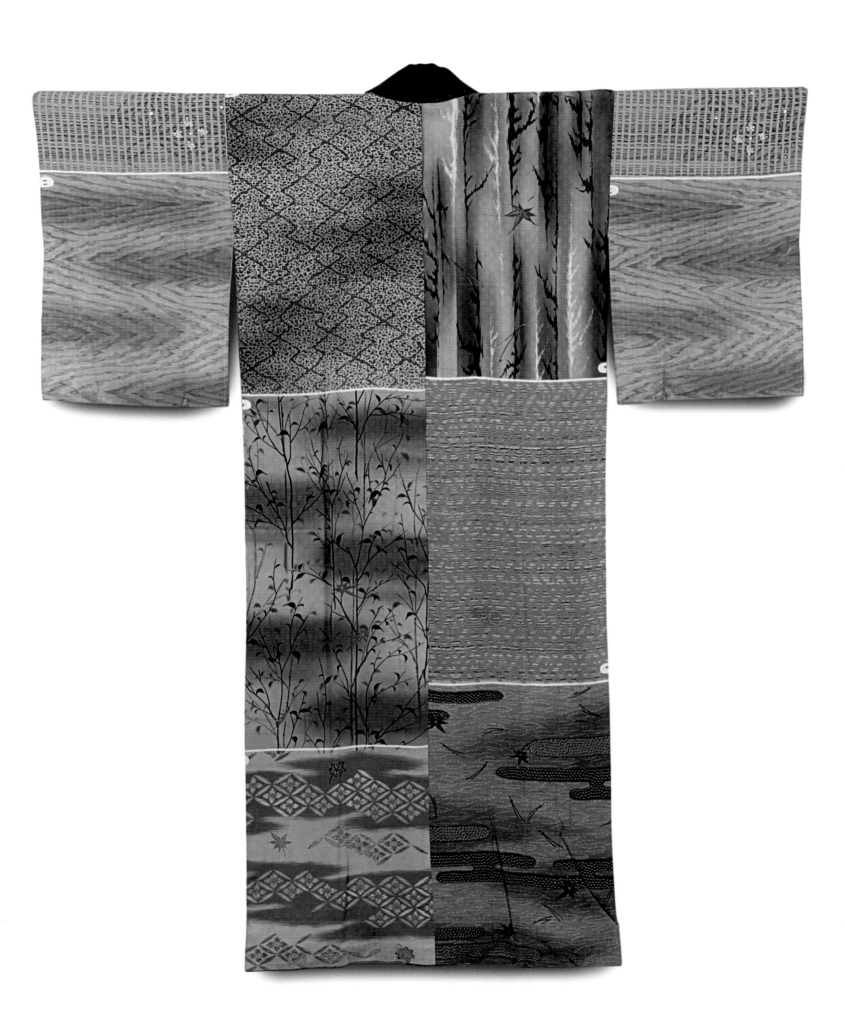

Women's Informal and Everyday Kimono
A Show of Modernity

32. Woodblock print *Tekagami* or 'hand-mirror' by Itō Shinsui (1898–1972), published by Watanabe Shōzaburō in 1954. Wessels Collection (Netherlands). The lady with a perm seems to be wearing a *meisen* kimono

33. Magnification of *meisen* fabric

Taishō had two faces: tradition and modernity. Both were reflected in the kimono of the 1920s and 1930s. Modernity can particularly be observed in everyday dress made of a relatively new type of raw silk (*futo-ori* or 'thick weave') and patterned in an *ikat* substitute technique: *meisen* kimono (cat. 24–32). These kimono were affordable for many women and therefore suitable vehicles for the rapidly changing designs and colours. Kimono entered the realm of seasonal fashion (fig. 32).

Meisen kimono were made of a thickly woven glossy fabric produced from raw or waste silk. This could be achieved thanks to the introduction of high frequency spinning machines, which were able to reduce the excess of floss lint. Due to several treatments during the production process, this kind of silk not only brought out the colours in a more brilliant way, it was more durable too.[1]

The decoration technique is related to *ikat* (in Japanese: *kasuri*). The effect was achieved by stencil dyeing of the warp threads prior to weaving (*hogushi-moyō*). For that purpose the warp threads were fixed on the loom and loosely held together with a temporary weft thread. Subsequently the threads were put on a long table. Making use of stencils, the whole length of the bolt was then dyed with a mixture of chemical pigments and rice paste: one stencil for each colour. After dyeing, the warp was transferred back to the loom for weaving. Due to the handling, some shifting of the threads inevitably occurred, which resulted in slightly blurred patterns, like in *ikat* (fig. 33). This technique was invented during the late nineteenth century. At the beginning of the twentieth

century, *meisen* with weft patterning (*yokoso-moyō*) or both warp and weft patterning (*heiyō-moyō*) could also be produced. The final product was a taffeta-like kimono with colourful repeating patterns over all the surface, and normally a cotton lining. *Meisen* kimono were not offered for sale as temporary sewn *karinui*, but as ready-made garments. Being informal dress, *meisen* kimono had no crests. The real craze for *meisen* developed after the 1923 Great Kantō Earthquake when most people in the Tokyo-Yokohama region had lost everything. Traditional kimono were much too expensive to restore women's wardrobes in the first years. As a result ready-made *meisen* kimono came under great demand, and it is not surprising that the production was concentrated in six regions of the Kantō plain around Tokyo.

Department stores picked up on the trade very quickly. Although the huge Mitsukoshi building at Nihonbashi with its entire stock of merchandise had been completely destroyed in the earthquake, a temporary store was already open on the compound of the old building six weeks later, and seven other temporary stores were erected at different locations in Tokyo soon after. Initially, *meisen* kimono were merely popular for their low price, but within a few years they became fashionable for their modern and colourful designs, which changed every season.

Geometrical designs became popular all over the world after the 1925 *Exposition des Arts Décoratifs et Industriels Modernes* in Paris. The rise of Art Deco therefore coincided with the rebuilding of Tokyo after the earthquake. The new fashion was part of the upswing of modernity in general during the reconstruction of the metropolis between 1923 and 1930.

Although *meisen* kimono certainly dominated the supply, other types of everyday dress were available as well. Coloured stripes in all kinds of variations had been in the repertoire of kimono decoration for centuries, and remained so during the early twentieth century. Equally popular remained kimono with tie-dye designs (*shibori*) and woven patterns. In the early Shōwa era, rayon (*jinken*) made its entry in Japan as an inexpensive alternative to silk.

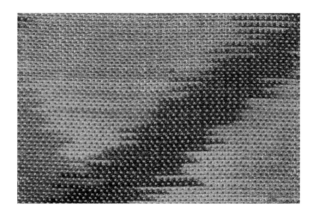

[1] Van Assche 1999: 30-39.

22. Stripes
Woman's kimono (no crests)
Outside: plain weave silk
Lining: red, white and golden-yellow silk
150 × 125 cm
1920–40

These woven vertical stripes (*shima*) in purple, blue and a golden yellow form the appealing design for this simple dress. Such designs were very common during the Meiji era.

23. Geometrical *shibori*
Woman's kimono (no crests)
Outside: fine crepe silk (*kinsha*);
damask weave with tie-dye decoration
(*shibori*)
Lining: red and old rose silk
150 × 126 cm
1920–40

Barely visible to the naked eye, the
fabric is a key-fret figured fine crepe.
Tie-dying with looped binding (*miura
shibori*) produced the black spots all
over the surface; subsequently the
geometrical areas have been dyed red,
yellow and blue.

24. View of the garden through leaded glass
Woman's kimono (no crests)
Outside: off-white silk; plain weave with stencil-printed warp and weft (*heiyō-gasuri meisen*)
Lining: red and pink cotton
152 × 123 cm
1920–40

It is not easy to decide what the subject matter of this kimono decoration is. Certainly flowering plants and trees can be observed within the framework of black lines. Are they leaded windows with parts of stained glass through which blurred views of the garden can be seen? The effect is comparable with that of the 'light screens' designed by Frank Lloyd Wright.

25. Colourful rectangles featuring geometrical patterns
Woman's kimono (no crests)
Outside: red silk; plain wave
with stencil-printed warp and weft
(*heiyō-gasuri meisen*)
Lining: white and purple-brown cotton
150 × 125 cm
1920–40

Meisen kimono were informal wear,
and therefore have no crests.
The technique required one screen
for each colour. In the *heiyō-gasuri*
technique both the warp and the weft
threads were stencil-dyed before
weaving.

26. Fantasy chrysanthemums
Woman's kimono (no crests)
Outside: grey-blue silk, plain
weave with stencil-printed weft
(*yokoso-gasuri meisen*)
Lining: white and pink cotton
151 × 128 cm
1920–40

27. Origami cranes and green camellias
Woman's kimono (no crests)
Outside: burgundy silk; plain
weave with stencil-printed warp
(*hogushi-gasuri meisen*)
Lining: white and cream cotton
146 × 118 cm
1920–40

The use of thicker weft threads
at 4 mm intervals provides this *meisen*
kimono with a finely ribbed texture.

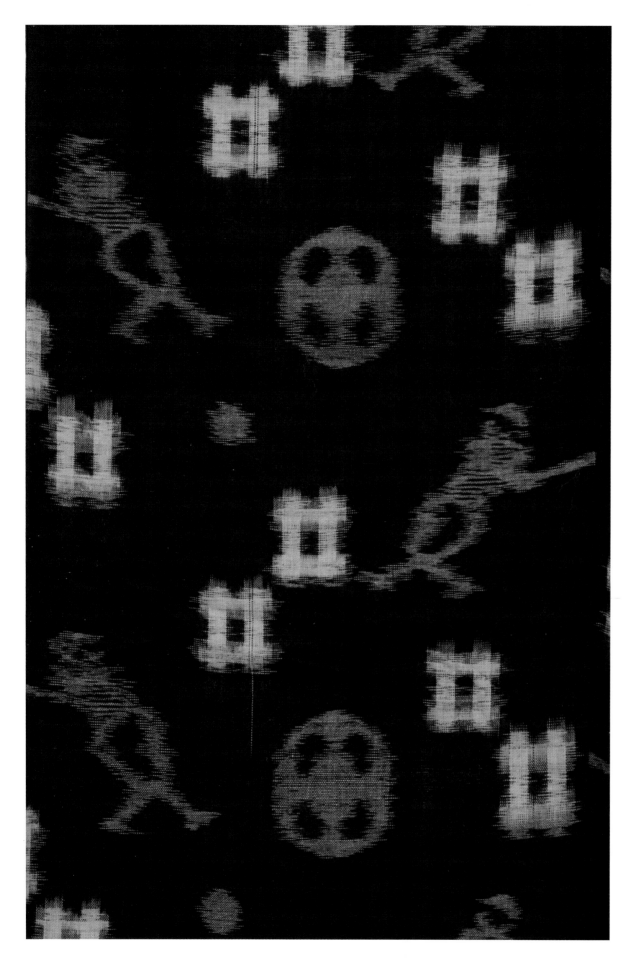

28. Baseball players
Woman's kimono (no crests)
Outside: indigo cotton; plain
weave with double ikat decoration
(*tateyoko-gasuri*)
Lining: white cotton at the shoulders
only
144 × 123 cm
1920–40

This machine-woven kimono,
manufactured in the Bingo area of
Hiroshima prefecture, shows a double
ikat design. Baseball players alternate
with balls.

29. Geometry
Woman's kimono (no crests)
Outside: ochre silk; plain weave
with stencil-printed weft (*yokoso-gasuri
meisen*)
Lining: white, salmon and red cotton
142 × 118 cm
1920–40

Geometrical designs became popular
in kimono design after the 1925
*Exposition des Arts Décoratifs et
Industriels Modernes* in Paris. The rise of
Art Deco coincided with the rebuilding
of the Tokyo metropolis after the
devastating 1923 Great Kantō
Earthquake. This coincidence provided
opportunities for modernity in kimono
manufacture: simple designs in serial
production.

30. Geometry and flowers
Woman's kimono (no crests)
Outside: off-white silk; plain
weave with stencil-printed weft
(*yokoso-gasuri meisen*)
Lining: white and salmon cotton
151 × 125 cm
1920–40

31. Roses

Woman's kimono (no crests)
Outside: purple silk; plain weave
with stencil-printed warp
(*hogushi-gasuri meisen*)
Lining: white and orange cotton
149 × 122 cm
1920–40

Geometrical designs and non-
indigenous flowers such as roses would
not have been appropriate for formal
wear.

32. Scattered small designs
Woman's kimono (no crests)
Outside: white silk; plain weave
with stencil-printed weft
(*yokoso-gasuri meisen*)
Lining: red and yellow synthetic fabric
149 × 124 cm
1930–50

Multicoloured and stylised
anthropomorphic and floral figures
are scattered over the ivory background
in groups divided by angled lines.

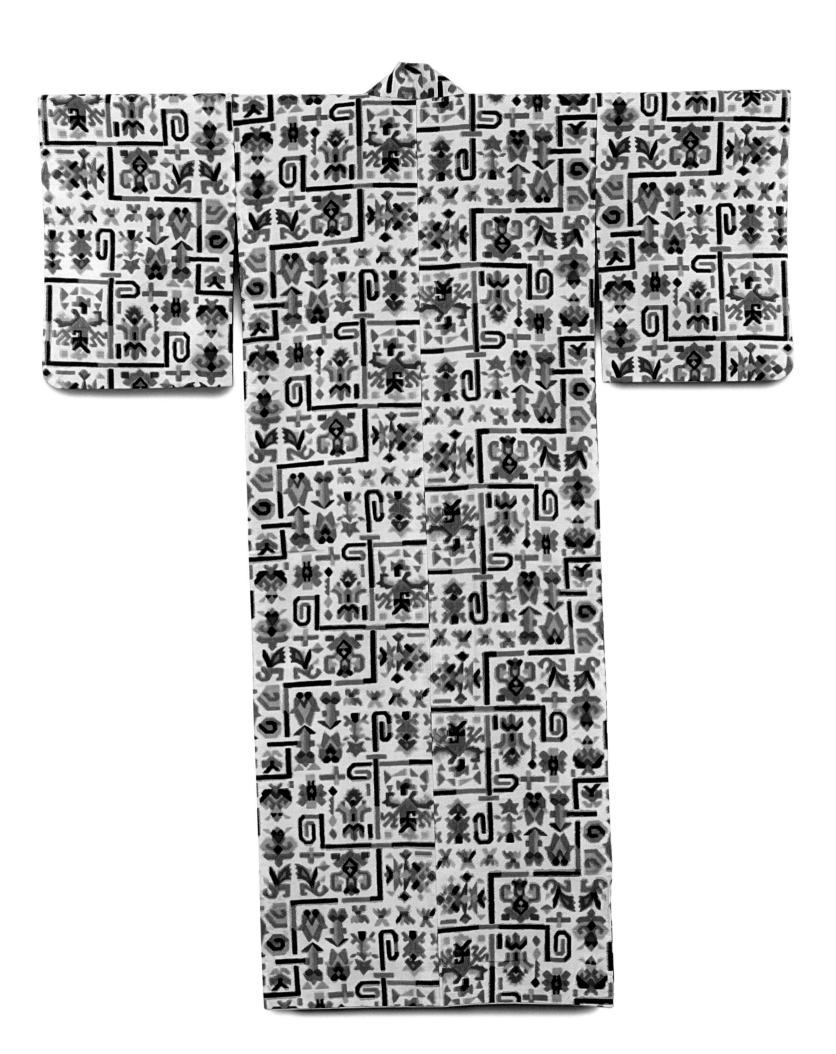

33. Black, blue and red lozenges
Woman's kimono (no crests)
Outside: fine crepe rayon (*jinken*)
Inside: cream cotton
148 × 119 cm
1920–40

Rayon or *jinken* is a manmade fibre of
natural cellulose from wood or cotton.
In 1883 Count Hilaire de Chardonnet
was the first to succeed in making this
semi-synthetic fabric, which he showed
at the 1889 World Fair in Paris.
Its industrial production only began
to flourish after 1920. One of the ways
to reduce the strong gloss of rayon
was by weaving over-twisted fibres into
a crepe fabric, like in this kimono.

Women's Jackets
The Masculine Touch

34. Magnification of *rinzu* damask weave

35. Interplay of the cranes in the damask weave silk and the *yūzen* decoration

Jackets or *haori* were not part of a woman's wardrobe until around 1895. As so often with fashion novelties, geisha had been the first to adopt this item of men's clothing. In the beginning only plain black *haori* with crests were worn on ceremonial occasions, but during the 1920s colourful designs came in vogue.

Taishō *haori* stand out for their elegant long sleeves and bodies. By that time the masculine connotation had already faded. All varieties of decoration techniques can be found in women's jackets: woven patterns, tie-dye, embroidery, *yūzen* in all its variants, *meisen*, etc. Special effects were achieved in the two *haori* of this collection, which were made of black gauze silk with a colourful *yūzen* decoration on the inside (cat. 35, 36). When worn, the design could only be perceived through the black gauze silk. Both jackets are of the expensive *musō haori* type, in which the inside and the outside have been made from the same fabric. The outer panels of the body continue uninterruptedly to the 'lining' – without seams at the lower ends (nor at the exterior of the shoulders). As a consequence *musō haori* have a centrefold seam inside. Damask-woven silk or *rinzu* was frequently used for

women's *haori*. It consisted of a monochrome patterned plain weave, in which the figures were created by making use of warp or weft floats and/or different thicknesses of the threads (fig. 34). This results in motifs of one colour, but different textures, which can best be discerned in changing light. Very often small repeating motifs were woven into the fabric, such as the key-fret pattern (*sayagata* – cat. 34), but also leaves and flowers were common. In some *haori*, the woven figures in the silk did not merely act as a background for the decoration, but as an intrinsic part of it. An example is the jacket with flying cranes; the birds are not only executed in *yūzen*, but also woven into the red silk (cat. 37, fig. 35).

During late Taishō and early Shōwa, a new fashion of designs woven from threads coated with red or green lacquer (*urushi*) in combination with silver or gold thread came up. Normally the designs were woven into black silk, which produced a subtle effect. The fashion continued after the war for several decades, and surprisingly remained limited to *haori*. Cat. 42 is a particularly eye-catching example due to the combination with brightly coloured tie-dye motifs of snow crystals.

34. Camellias
Woman's *haori* (no crests)
Outside: red fine crepe silk (*kinsha*);
damask weave (*rinzu*) with
stencil-printed, direct-dye method
decoration (*kata-yūzen*)
Inside: plain weave silk with
stencil-printed decoration
124 × 99 cm
1920–40

Camellias were among the most
popular motifs in the Taishō period.
As one of the first flowers in the new
year they were hailed as forebodings
of spring. On this *haori* the camellias
are harmoniously spread over the
key-fret (*sayagata*) figured silk
background. The lining shows
spinning tops.
Characteristic of the period are the
three-quarters bodice and long sleeves.

35. The calligrapher and the frog

Woman's *musō haori* (three crests)
Outside: black silk, gauze weave (*ro*)
Crest: oak (*kashiwa*)
Lining: silk; hand-painted with
rice-paste resist outlining (*yūzen*),
embroidery and silver thread
129 × 105 cm
1920–40

Ono no Tōfū (894–966) is considered
the founder of Japanese calligraphy.
In early life his writing was so
indifferent that he failed several times
in his efforts for advancement at court.
However, one day while he was crossing
a bridge during a Summer shower,
he noticed a frog endeavouring to jump
onto an overhanging willow branch.
Over and over again the little animal
jumped, only to fall back again, until
at last, nearly exhausted, it succeeded in
catching a leaf, and climbed the branch.
This lesson in perseverance encouraged
Tōfū to return to his task, ultimately
arriving at the height of his ambition.[1]
In this *musō haori*, the lining is not
separately attached to the jacket, but is
part of its structure. The willow spreads
over both the bodice and the sleeves,
and, due to the transparent gauze-
weave, can be perceived through the
outer layer, both from the front and the
back. The stream is even more visible as
the result of the addition of a few silver
threads.
Tōfū as a young man in court dress
carrying an umbrella is watching the
attempts of the frog to catch hold of
the wet willow tree. The hat of the
courtier, details of his robe and
raindrops on the willow have been
embroidered.

[1] Edmunds (n.d.): 628-29.

36. Autumn grasses
Woman's *musō haori* (three crests)
Outside: black gauze weave silk (*ro*);
damask weave (*rinzu*)
Crest: melon (*mokko*)
Lining: black gauze weave silk (*ro*);
hand-painted with rice-paste resist
outlining (*yūzen*)
124 × 90 cm
1920–40

Like the previous jacket, this is a *musō haori*, which means that the outside and inside were made from the same bolt of silk: the seamless front and back panels continue to the lining.
As an additional refinement, the black gauze weave of this jacket was made of figured satin (damask weave) with a pattern of grasses and dewdrops. Therefore the colourful autumn herbs on the inside are not merely observed from the outside through a black gauze, but seem to grow in a dense field of dark grasses. The *yūzen* decoration was carried out with meticulous grading of the colours.

37. White and red cranes

Woman's *haori* (one crest)
Outside: pink silk, damask weave (*rinzu*); hand-painted with rice-paste resist outlining (*yūzen*) and gold foil additions
Crest: flower diamond (*hanabishi*)
Lining: silk; damask weave (*rinzu*) with stencil-printed decoration
125 × 96 cm
1920–40

A lively design of flying cranes, both in and on the silk. Furthermore, origami cranes adorn the lining.

38. 'Parting at dawn'

Woman's *haori* (three crests)
Outside: black fine crepe silk (*kinsha*), damask weave (*rinzu*); hand-painted with rice-paste resist outlining (*yūzen*) and some embroidery; basting stitches still present
Crest: snake's eyes (*janome*)
Lining: red fine crepe silk (*kinsha*); hand-painted with rice-paste resist outlining (*yūzen*) and gold foil application
125 × 93 cm
1920–40

An ox carriage – a vehicle used by the aristocracy in the Heian period – stands by a stream in the middle of a pine forest. Also a pair of boxes for the shell game (*kaoike*) testifies to human presence. Several pines are grown over with wisteria or vine. In between the pines a few maples and flowering cherries, on the ground chrysanthemums, bamboo, reeds and grasses. The tree trunks are invisible: it seems to be night. The lining is adorned with a crowing rooster announcing daybreak. All image elements together seem to depict the Barrier of Osaka, where lovers secretly met in Heian times. In her *Pillow Book*, Sei Shōnagon alludes to this theme:

> There may be some who are deceived
> By the cock's crow that falsely breaks
> The stillness of the night.
> But such a fraud will not beguile
> The Barrier of Osaka
> Where lovers have their trysts.

Translation by Ivan Morris
(Morris 1967: 154)

39. Flowering plum and bamboo
Woman's *haori* (no crests)
Outside: beige fine crepe silk (*kinsha*)
with stencil-printed, direct-dye
decoration (*kata-yūzen*)
Lining: fine crepe silk (*kinsha*) with
stencil-printed decoration and gold foil
application
126 × 92 cm
1920–40

40. Fans and flowers
Woman's *haori* (no crests)
Outside: burgundy fine crepe silk
(*kinsha*) with imitation embroidery
(*nuitori shishū*)
Lining: white silk, damask weave
(*rinzu*)
128 × 83 cm
1920–40

Nuitori shishū is a weaving technique
that simulates embroidery.

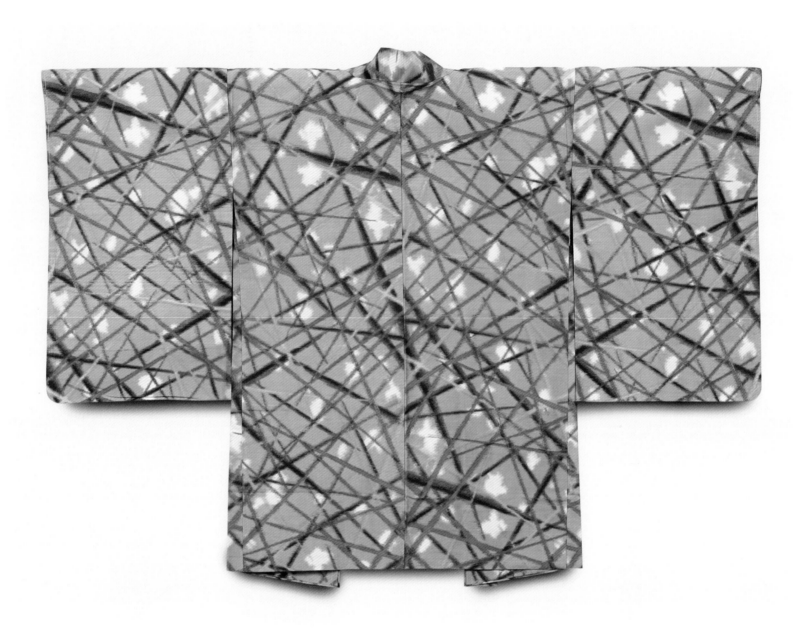

41. Coloured lines
Woman's *haori* (no crests)
Outside: beige silk; plain weave
with stencil-printed weft (*yokoso-gasuri
meisen*); basting stitches still present
Inside: plain weave silk with
stencil-printed decoration
124 × 84 cm
1920–40

Could the design be an impression
of New Year fireworks in the snow?

42. Snow crystals
Woman's *haori* (one crest)
Outside: black fine crepe silk (*kinsha*)
with tie-dye (*shibori*) and
supplementary weft
Crest: *katabami* (wood sorrel)
Lining: plain weave silk with
stencil-printed decoration
124 × 88 cm
1920–40

Sometimes traditional motifs match
well with modernity, such as in this
jacket with bold snow crystals, some
worked in very fine *shibori*, others in
supplementary weft of fine flat gold,
silver and lacquered strips. Especially
attractive is the *ton-sur-ton* black crystal
on the back.

Men's Jackets
Hidden Stories

36. Large size *katagami* stencil made of impregnated layers of mulberry paper (however *katagami* used for *kata-yūzen* had numerous small perforations). Author's collection

37. Close-up of the Ōshima *tsumugi* fabric with hexagonal 'turtle shell' pattern of cat. 53

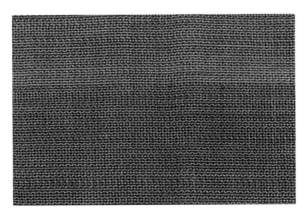

In comparison with women's kimono, little has been written on men's dress. Men's outer kimono were not decorated, but made of plain black, dark blue, dark green or dark grey silk. The quality of the silk showed considerable variations, from smooth glossy black *habutae* silk to dull raw *tsumugi* silk with an attractive coarse texture. Decoration, however, was reserved for two other garments: the under-kimono and the lining of the jacket.

At least in part, such forbearance of outward display must have been the result of the sumptuary edicts, which were issued time and time again during the Tokugawa period. In this way, the shogunate tried to restrict urban frivolity and luxurious living by the common people, in particular of the rising merchant class. They were forbidden to wear silk or to display themselves in extravagant clothing. In order to comply superficially to the regime's instructions, merchants often appeared in simple cotton kimono with richly adorned silk undergarments. Such concealed luxury seems to have added to their inner pride. Even when they were no longer obliged to after the 1868 Meiji Restoration, well-to-do men continued their habit of wearing apparently austere dress with hidden luxury underneath.

Apart from the occasional exception in *tsutsugaki-yūzen*, most *haori* linings were done in either stencil-printed *kata-yūzen* or in multicoloured brocade weave, which often included gold and silver thread (*nishiki*).

Kata-yūzen had been invented by Hirose Jisuke around 1879. A mixture of dyes with rice paste (*utsushi-nori*) was directly painted on the textile through the holes of the stencils (*katagami*), which were intricately cut out of impregnated mulberry paper (fig. 36). For each colour one stencil was required. These could be used repeatedly, often twenty or thirty times. In this way designs could be produced in multiples, so reducing the costs.

Brocade-weaving (*nishiki*) had been much improved following the introduction of the Jacquard loom in 1873. After the adaptation of the patterning mechanism to the wooden Japanese draw-loom, the production of complex silk brocades in multiples became easier too. Sometimes rectangular decorated panels were just sewn into the lining of a jacket (cat. 43, 44), but more often the lining of both the body and the sleeves constituted a whole (cat. 48, 49, 52). The decoration was mostly limited to the back, but sometimes it continued in damask weave to the sleeves (cat. 53, 57). In contrast to women's *haori*, the sleeves of men's jackets were fully connected to the bodies without leaving openings. Among the themes of decoration, fierce animals and the Gods of Good Fortune were very popular. Topics related to theatre, classical literature, the tea ceremony and history reflect a leaning toward tradition. Contemporary subjects such as a baseball match and the birth of the crown prince are among the most intriguing ones (cat. 63, 62). One lining in this collection is related to the contemporary Nihonga style of painting (cat. 61). Very common were combinations of cartouches (either rectangular or in the shape of a fan or a snow crystal) filled with colourful pictures against a more subdued, shaded background.

The degree of formality of a jacket was decided by the kind of fabric from which it was made and by the number of crests. Only black and glossy *habutae* silk – plain weave, shiny and rather thick – was used for ceremonial wear. Such jackets always had five crests, but were not necessarily more expensive than raw silk jackets without crests (fig. 37).

43. Daruma dolls

Man's *haori* (five crests)
Outside: black *habutae* silk
Crest: plum (*ume*)
Lining: silk with stencil-printed,
direct-dye decoration (*kata-yūzen*)
and gold leaf remnants
133 × 107 cm
1910–30

Legend has it that the Indian sage
Bodhidharma (in Japanese: Daruma)
founded Zen Buddhism in China, and
brought it subsequently to Japan in the
sixth century.
Daruma is said to have lost his arms
and legs after nine years of meditation
in a cave. At temple markets, papier-
mâché dolls representing Daruma were
sold without pupils in their eyes.
The customer painted one pupil while
making a wish and added the other
pupil once the wish had been fulfilled.
In the sixteenth century such dolls were
called *okiagari koboshi* or 'the little
priest who stands up', since they
returned to their original position when
tipped over. The inscription on the
jacket refers to this feature: "Never falls
down, never falls down, even after cups
of alcohol he never falls down".
The signature and seal could not be
identified.
A similar *haori* with identical first part
of the inscription has been published
in *Arts of Asia* (2006), vol. 36, no. 4,
p. 52, fig. 11.

44. Hotei and his sack, framed by a flaming pearl
Man's *haori* (five crests)
Outside: black *habutae* silk
Crest: falcon's feathers (*takanoha*)
Lining: silk with stencil-printed, direct-dye decoration (*kata-yūzen*)
Inscription: Sesshū
125 × 105 cm
1910–30

Hotei is one of the seven Gods of Good Fortune. He is usually depicted with his large bag full of precious things, and often surrounded by children, who are trying to find out the contents of the bag. Hotei is considered the God of Contentment and Happiness – but not on this *haori*. Here he seems to be fed up with all that good fortune, despite being shown within the Wish-Granting Pearl (*tama*) as a cartouche. The *sumie* black ink painting is signed Sesshū. Sesshū Tōyō (1420–1506) was the most famous *sumie* painter from the Muromachi era, and was known for his strong brushstrokes.
The lining of this *haori* is spotted with blue dyestuff as if the colour had been running after washing. In addition, the red seal under the signature has almost entirely been cut away. Has the lining perhaps been used more than one time in several *haori*?

45. Ebisu and Daikoku in a boat harvesting seaweed
Man's *haori* (five crests)
Outside: black *habutae* silk
Crest: fans (*ōgi*)
Lining: silk with stencil-printed, direct-dye decoration (*kata-yūzen*)
133 × 101 cm
1920–40

Ebisu (standing) and Daikoku (squatting) are two other Gods of Good Fortune. Here they are shown in a boat harvesting plants (possibly seaweed) with a sickle, although they are normally depicted fishing treasures. In the background the heavily laden Treasure Ship or *takarabune* is depicted. Several of these treasures are scattered among the characters on the background.
In the book *Fashioning Kimono* an identical lining, erroneously described as brocade-woven (no. 35), has been published.[1] The inscription was deciphered as: "The business went well with this boat, becoming a treasure ship". The fact that the linings are identical implies that they were made using the same screens.

[1] Van Assche 2005: 136, 140-41.

46. Dragon in swirling clouds
Man's *haori* (five crests)
Outside: black *habutae* silk
Crest: ivy (*tsuta*)
Lining: brocade-woven silk (*nishiki*)
130 × 102 cm
1920–40

In ancient times, the Chinese dragon was primarily a rain and fertility symbol. Therefore the dragon was often depicted in heavy clouds and often accompanied by lightning. Later this supernatural being became associated with the emperor. The Chinese described it as deaf, having the head of a camel, horns of a deer, scales of a carp and paws of a tiger. The number of claws was regulated: for the emperor five, for the nobles four and for the common people three. In Japan, dragons have normally three claws. It was believed that the dragon was horrified by the sight of a piece of silk dyed in five colours, possibly because this resembled the rainbow: an announcement that the sun would soon drive away the rain clouds. The text is a quotation by Saigō Takamori (1827–77) from *The Book of Later Han*: "Men of high ambition must comport themselves with the same degree of manliness". Saigō Takamori was one of the heroes of the Meiji Restoration, and a student of Confucianism in his youth.

47. Tigers running in the snow
Man's *haori* (five crests)
Outside: black *habutae* silk
Crest: oak (*kashiwa*)
Lining: brocade-woven silk (*nishiki*)
129 × 100 cm
1920–40

Whereas the dragon was considered the strongest animal in heaven, the tiger was the strongest animal on earth. Both animals were often illustrated together, as symbols of spring and autumn, the male and female principles, rain and wind, etc.

When a tiger became 500 years old its fur turned white, but the white fur on the bellies of the tigers on this *haori* is due to the snow.

Since tigers were not indigenous to Japan, they were not depicted in a naturalistic way until the Meiji era (1868–1912), when contacts with other nations became regular. The heads of the tigers on this woven lining are in between the traditional rendition and naturalism.

As tigers live solitary lives, this pair may represent immature siblings from the same nest, playfully running in the fresh snow. The ivory background creates a subtle contrast with the thick white snowflakes. Several details, such as the eyes and the teeth, are woven in gold.

**48. Tiger hiding in bamboo
under the crescent moon**
Man's *haori* (one stitched crest)
Outside: black raw silk (*tsumugi*)
Crest: oak (*kashiwa*)
Lining: brocade-woven silk (*nishiki*)
131 × 103 cm
1920–40

The tiger on this lining looks much
more naturalistic than the pair on the
previous *haori*. Note the larger size
of its head.
The association of bamboo with a tiger
is a traditional one, and symbolic of
the shelter the strong sometimes seek
among the weak.
The tiger is clearly visible in the
moonlight, but the blurring of the
green bamboo towards the edge of the
image intensifies the feeling of night.
The jacket has only one crest on the
middle of the back, indicating its use
as a rather informal article of clothing.

49. Wan Xizhi, Wang Xianzhi and the Orchid Pavilion

Man's *haori* (no crests)
Outside: dark brown raw silk (*tsumugi*)
Lining: brocade-woven silk (*nishiki*)
131 × 106 cm
1920–40

Wan Xizhi (303–61 AD) was a Chinese calligrapher, famous for his *Lan Ting Xu* ('Preface to the collection of poems composed at the Orchid pavilion'), in which he described a summer outing of poets. The original manuscript was lost, only the rubbings of stone tablets with his calligraphy remain.

On the lining of this jacket the figures of Wan Xizhi (in Japan known as Ōgishi) and his son Wan Xianzhi (known as Ōhinshi) are woven in two monochrome colours against a dark brown background. They can only be seen clearly when the angle of the light changes. Wan Xianzhi is making ink on an ink stone, whereas his father is painting the text on the smooth face of a rock. The figures themselves are woven in such a way as to simulate a painting. Everything on this lining seems to be related with ink.

On the fan, the Orchid Pavilion is 'painted' in a beautiful landscape, which in reality is woven in black, red-brown, green, silver and gold against an ivory background. Some 'wear' of the fan can be observed at the places where it is attached to the ribs.

50. Torn fan paintings and part of a gold screen

Man's *haori* (five crests)
Outside: black *habutae* silk
Crest: well crib and stripes (*igeta* and *hikiryo*)
Lining: silk with stencil-printed, direct-dye decoration (*kata-yūzen*), additional hand-painting and gold leaf application
132 × 102 cm
1920–40

Two frayed fans, showing scenes from classical literature, are lying on top of a larger frayed fragment of a gold-leaf screen or sliding door with a peasant on a raft and a calligraphic text. The decoration has a beautiful gradation of colours and at many places gold leaf has been applied, such as on the hat of the courtier and on the roof. The faces of the figures and also the peasant were hand-painted.

The scenes on the fans could well be derived from the *Genji monogatari*, written by the court lady Murasaki Shikibu around the year 1008. 'The Tale of Genji' is considered the first great novel in world literature. It narrates the life and loves of Prince Genji in the refined circles of the court and nobility in Kyoto of the Heian period (794–1185). The work has greatly influenced all kinds of Japanese art throughout the centuries. Here the court ladies have been rendered as stout, cheerful figures in their typically multi-layered dress and extremely long hair. On the upper fan the courtier is listening to the *koto* music played by the lady, on the lower fan several ladies seem to enjoy the coolness of the fast-flowing brook under the platform.

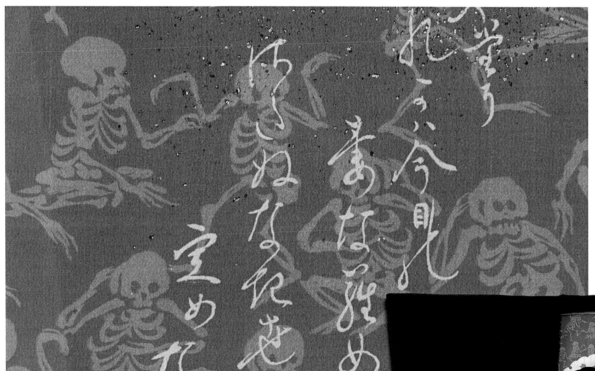

51. Geisha and skeletons

Man's *haori* (no crests)
Outside: black *tsumugi* silk
Lining: silk with stencil-printed,
direct-dye decoration (*kata-yūzen*)
132 × 100 cm
1920–40

Ikkyū Sōjun (1392-1481) was an
eccentric Zen priest, who spent more
time in brothels and wine shops than
in temples and hermitages. He was
a noted poet and calligrapher, but also
published several prose pieces that
denounced hypocrisy in religious
matters. His most famous text is
Gaikotsu ('Skeletons'). Its message that
humans are nothing but skeletons
dressed in skin has been depicted on
the lining of this *haori*. The two snow
crystal roundels – symbolic of the
transient character of things – show the
images of geisha: in one crystal we see
two geisha in colour, in the other, a
gloomy black figure. The background is
filled with dancing and music-making
skeletons, who seem to be happier than
the melancholic geisha. Scattered flakes
of gold-leaf enhance the reflection.
All elements of this picture, including
the poem, were also observed on a
man's under-kimono, but arranged
in a different way over a larger surface.
This shows how stencils of picture
elements can be used for the creation
of a new composition.

52. Playing puppies and a poem
Man's *haori* (five crests)
Outside: black *habutae* silk
Crest: well crib (*igeta*)
Lining: brocade-woven silk (*nishiki*)
131 × 107 cm
1920–40

This lining has a brocade-woven decoration of three puppies playing against a beautiful green background. The inscription is a text by the Zen monk Shaku Sōen (1859–1919), who travelled widely in Ceylon and India. In 1893 and in 1905–06 he lectured in the United States and held the first *zazen* meditation session there.
The text about puppies, the priest Jōshū and a bowl of soup is rather mysterious, and probably requires a spark of enlightenment to enable its understanding. Dogs were sometimes considered reincarnations of the Buddha. The signature reads: Ryōgakutsu Sōen.
This lining has interesting textures: the white parts feel rough, whereas the very smooth gold areas are slightly depressed in the green background.

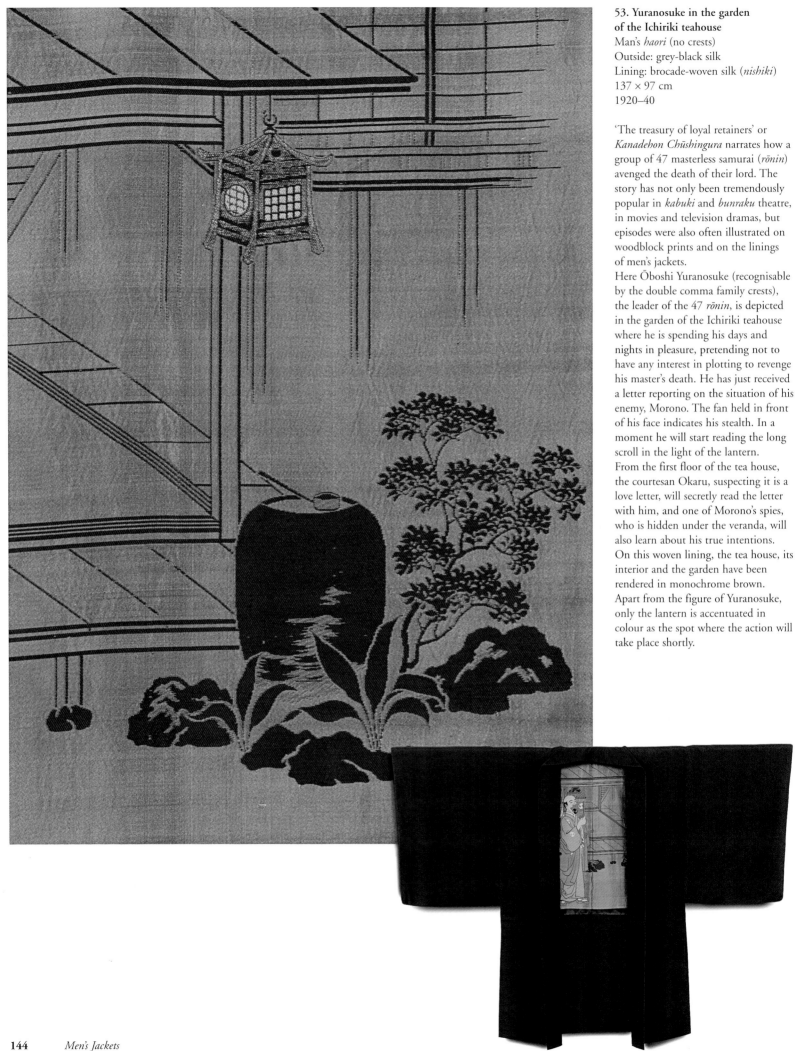

53. Yuranosuke in the garden of the Ichiriki teahouse

Man's *haori* (no crests)
Outside: grey-black silk
Lining: brocade-woven silk (*nishiki*)
137 × 97 cm
1920–40

'The treasury of loyal retainers' or *Kanadehon Chūshingura* narrates how a group of 47 masterless samurai (*rōnin*) avenged the death of their lord. The story has not only been tremendously popular in *kabuki* and *bunraku* theatre, in movies and television dramas, but episodes were also often illustrated on woodblock prints and on the linings of men's jackets.

Here Ōboshi Yuranosuke (recognisable by the double comma family crests), the leader of the 47 *rōnin*, is depicted in the garden of the Ichiriki teahouse where he is spending his days and nights in pleasure, pretending not to have any interest in plotting to revenge his master's death. He has just received a letter reporting on the situation of his enemy, Morono. The fan held in front of his face indicates his stealth. In a moment he will start reading the long scroll in the light of the lantern. From the first floor of the tea house, the courtesan Okaru, suspecting it is a love letter, will secretly read the letter with him, and one of Morono's spies, who is hidden under the veranda, will also learn about his true intentions. On this woven lining, the tea house, its interior and the garden have been rendered in monochrome brown. Apart from the figure of Yuranosuke, only the lantern is accentuated in colour as the spot where the action will take place shortly.

54. Kaoru and the letter

Man's *haori* (no crests)
Outside: Ōshima *tsumugi*
Lining: brocade-woven silk (*nishiki*)
and damask weave (*rinzu*)
129 × 103 cm
1920–40

An elegant lady, dressed in a blue kimono decorated with gold waterwheels and with a hairstyle that suggests a Genroku-period beauty, is leaning out of the circular window, contemplating a letter. A pair of glasses lies on top of the letter.

The figured satin lining of the sleeves with lanterns, double comma motifs and fishing nets hanging to dry reveals that the subject of the decoration is the *Chūshingura* – the same as in the previous jacket. The lady must then be Okaru, who had agreed to be sold by her father as a courtesan to the Gion pleasure district to provide funds to Kampei, one of the heroes. She has just grasped that the letter which Yuranosuke read in the light of the lantern was not a love letter, but a report on their common enemy Morono's situation. Now she understands that Yuranosuke is still loyal to the cause of his late master. This lining depicts the scene after the one shown in cat. 53.

The weaving exhibits fine detailing, such as the rouge in the lady's face, the writings on the letter and the glass in the pair of spectacles.

Tsumugi is a plain weave fabric made of hand-twisted silk filaments from hatched cocoons. The uneven thickness of the yarns produces a pleasant texture (see fig. 37). Ōshima, where this particular kind of *tsumugi* was produced, is one of the Amami Islands halfway between Kyūshū and Okinawa.

55. Yūya and the Kiyomizu temple

Man's *haori* (five crests)
Outside: black *habutae* silk
Crest: ivy (*tsuta*)
Lining: brocade-woven silk (*nishiki*)
130 × 105 cm
1920–40

Yūya was the mistress of Taira no Munemori, one of the leaders in the Taira-Minamoto War (1180–85). Her old mother repeatedly requested for Yūya to be sent home for a while, that she might see her before she died. But Munemori didn't want her to leave Kyoto until the festive flower-viewing season was over. It all turned to sadness. The woven lining shows a masked *nō* actor in the role of Yūya reading her mother's letter. In the background the silvery silhouette of the Kiyomizu temple is surrounded by the wooded hills of Higashiyama.
The poem reads:

Butterflies are wavering around the flowers.
Snow flies and
Bush warblers fly above willows.
Pieces of gold:
Flowers floating on the stream

花前
は蝶
群小
　　
　　
紛々
と
雪
柳
　　
上は
鶯
と
ふ
月
く
　　
雪
金
花
八
流
水

56. Sailing ships

Man's *musō haori* (one stitched crest)
Outside: black raw silk (*tsumugi*)
Crest: wisteria (*fuji*)
Lining: silk; hand-painted with rice-paste resist outlining (*yūzen*)
131 × 100 cm
1920–40

Musō jackets, which have linings from the same fabric as the outside, were more costly than *haori* with inset decorated linings, and the *tsumugi* fabric must have made it even more expensive. Nevertheless, a *haori* not cut out of glossy silk was unsuitable for ceremonial occasions. The unobtrusive stitched shadow crest (*kage mon*) corresponds with the low grade of formality of this jacket.

On close inspection, one can observe that the boats were hand-painted. The background continues onto the lining of the sleeves. The sailing ships seem to be fifteenth- or sixteenth-century vessels. The gun-holes suggest that they are of foreign origin.

57. 'Hideyoshi's patience'

Man's *haori* (no crests)
Outside: brown raw silk (*tsumugi*)
Lining: brocade-woven silk (*nishiki*) and
damask weave (*rinzu*)
132 × 92 cm
1920–40

Hideyoshi no tintai or 'Hideyoshi's patience' is the title of this woven lining, as can be read at the bottom. It is a scene from *Taikōki* or 'Chronicles of the Regent', of which several variants have been published, the most important one by Oze Hoan (1564–1640), not long after Hiheyoshi's death. Toyotomi Hideyoshi (1537–98) was the warlord who completed the reunification of Japan after more than a century of civil war. According to *Taikōki*, Katsuie and Morimasa tried to teach the short-tempered Hideyoshi the importance of being more flexible and patient. This must be the subject of the council of generals, in which the young Hideyoshi seems to give Katsuie a massage (both can be identified by the crests on their dress). A free interpretation of Hideyoshi's family crest has been woven into the figured satin lining of the sleeves.

Although the subject matter is traditional, this picture does not seem to be derived from an old book illustration or print, since it features a kind of perspective (note the decreasing size of the motifs on the sliding doors) and also clear-dark grading (*chiaroscuro*) in the clothing of the figures. Therefore it is more likely that the picture was derived from a Meiji oil-painting.

The quality of the weaving is very sophisticated, such as in the dragon on the gold screen at the top right.

58. The tea pavilion
Man's *haori* (five crests)
Outside: black *habutae* silk
Crest: comma pattern (*tomoe*)
Lining: brocade-woven silk (*nishiki*)
128 × 98 cm
1920–40

The worn silvery fan features a river landscape. A small pavilion is hidden under the trees on the right bank. A standing figure is watching the scenery. The whole simulates a monochrome painting, only the pavilion is highlighted by a few colour accents. The top and bottom borders are woven in intricate patterns. Furthermore, there is a wonderful brocade bag for a tea caddy and a porcelain incense container decorated with a landscape.

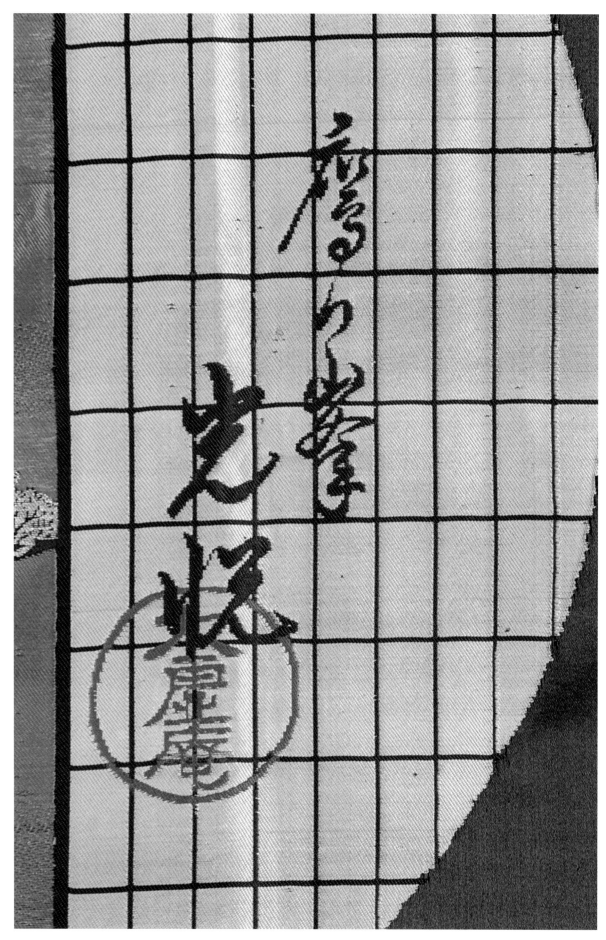

Man's haori (five crests)
Outside: black *habutae* silk
Crest: handle (*kan*)
Lining: brocade-woven silk (*nishiki*)
128 × 98 cm
1920–40

The half-open sliding doors offer a view
of the distant mountains. Above the
mountains a poem by Fujiwara
Toshinari (1114–1204) has been woven
in the lining:

> There is no escape from the suffering
> in this world
> Even in the deep forest, the deer's
> sad voice is heard

The paper sliding doors show the
inscription: 'Tagamine Kōetsu
Daikyoan'. Hon'ami Kōetsu
(1558–1637) was a famous calligrapher,
potter and designer of lacquer objects
and printed books. In 1615 he founded
a small community of craftsmen called
Tagamine; Daikyoan was the small
temple of this village. Kōetsu had a
great interest in the tea ceremony: the
tea bowl on this lining may have been
made by himself, and its decoration
inspired by the view. In the right upper
part a tea spoon and its container are
depicted.

60. Daily life in Edo

Man's *haori* (no crests)
Outside: black raw silk (*tsumugi*)
Lining: brocade-woven silk (*nishiki*)
and damask weave (*rinzu*)
132 × 89 cm
1920–40

Decorated squares, circles and fan-
shapes are commonly found on *haori*
linings. Here they are placed against the
silhouette of a river with two bridges
and some buildings on the far bank.
Within the three rectangles scenes from
daily life of the Edo period are
depicted: countrywomen carrying
faggots on a mountain path below
Mount Fuji, women collecting shells on
the shore, and people preparing dough.

61. 'A study of elegance'

Man's *haori* (five crests)
Outside: black *habutae* silk
Crest: seven treasures and flower
diamond (*shippō* and *hanabishi*)
Lining: silk with stencil-printed,
direct-dye decoration (*kata-yūzen*) with
additional hand-painting; unidentified
seal
123 × 80 cm
1920–40

On the floor of the room lies a book
entitled *Furyu kenkyū* or 'A study of
elegance'. The pensive lady in a loose
gown is leaning against the railing.
She has opened the sliding doors, and
therefore the treetops outside can be
seen. One of the bamboo blinds is
lowered. On the left side, part of a large
square panel can be observed. What is
it? A painter's easel? Is the lady a
painter?
The style of the image on this lining
reflects the often slightly sentimental
Nihonga style of the early twentieth
century. Unfortunately, the designer's
seal has not yet been identified.

62. Emperor Akihito's birth

Man's *haori* (five crests)
Outside: black *habutae* silk
Crest: wood sorrel (*katabami*)
Lining: silk with stencil-printed, direct-dye decoration (*kata-yūzen*) and hand-painted additions
127 × 95 cm
Late 1933 or early 1934

It rarely happens that a kimono can be dated exactly, but this *haori* is one such example. The newspapers depicted on the lining announce the birth of an heir to the throne on 23 December, Shōwa 8 (equivalent of 1933). Within the circle, Nijūbashi – the bridge to the imperial palace in Tokyo – is illustrated with the equestrian statue of the heroic samurai Kunosuke Masashige (1294–1336). Young boys are often associated with samurai in the hope that they will become as brave and strong as a warrior in the future. Crowds carrying the national flag rejoice in the birth of the long awaited prince.

Pressure had already been put on Emperor Hirohito to take concubines in order to produce a son, and it was rumoured that he had already played cards with a candidate – in the presence of the empress, of course.[2] It was therefore more than welcome, that the empress finally gave birth to Tsugu no Miya – the present emperor Akihito. The map not only shows Japan but also Korea, since this country had been annexed in 1910. The many railways, the warships and the biplanes reflect the strongly nationalistic mood in Japan in the 1930s. The political and military developments, especially with regard to China, were already getting out of hand.

[2] Bix 2001: 271.

63. The baseball match
Man's *haori* (five crests)
Outside: black *habutae* silk
Crest: hexagon and flower diamond
(*kikkō* and *hanabishi*)
Lining: silk with stencil-printed,
direct-dye decoration (*kata-yūzen*)
129 × 101 cm
1920–40

Baseball is the most popular team sport in Japan, and was first played at *Keisei gakkō* (now Tokyo University) in 1873. Around 1900, baseball clubs were formed in middle schools throughout the country. The annual series between Keiō University and Waseda University, the foremost intercollegiate rivalry, started in 1903. Due to fan rows, the Keiō-Waseda games were discontinued in 1906, and only resumed in 1925. Following World War II the two old rivals played the first baseball match within three months of Japan's surrender. In 2003, the 100th anniversary of the Keiō-Waseda games was celebrated with a match won by Keiō.

The lining of this jacket shows a match from the viewpoint of a spectator from behind chicken wire. The club has been thrown on the ground, the ball is probably in the hand of the white Keiō catcher at the home-base. The name of the opposing blue team is not mentioned. Must be Waseda! No doubt the jacket belonged to a Keiō-team supporter.

64. Festive harvesting time around Mount Fuji

Man's *haori* (five crests)
Outside: black *habutae* silk; company mark 'Kimura' at the lower end of the right lapel
Crest: wood sorrel (*katabami*)
Lining: brocade-woven silk (*nishiki*)
133 × 100 cm
1920–40

The countryside is bathed in golden sunlight, with a breath of air that enables threshing. The couple has been working since the early morning, several chickens try to get their share of the grains. Tall trees supply some shade to the thatched farmhouse. Clothes are hanging to dry on the line, a car is being parked between the house and the shed, flowers are blooming on the bank of the stream. Snow-topped Mount Fuji dominates the scenery. It may be a national holiday, since the flag is out. The patterns on the lining of the sleeves may suggest water, which is abundant around Mount Fuji. This brocade-woven lining is extremely rich in detail.

65. Cormorant fishing at Arashiyama
Man's *haori* (no crests)
Outside: dark grey, slightly textured silk
Lining: brocade-woven silk (*nishiki*)
134 × 97 cm
1920–40

Night-time at Arashiyama, the mountains in Western Kyoto, where *ukai* cormorant fishing is still practised on the Katsura River. Especially on moonless nights the fish are easily attracted by fires in the iron baskets. Cormorants on long leashes catch *ayu*, a sweet fish, but they are prevented from swallowing the catch due to the metal rings around their necks.
Within the rectangle a lively depiction of the fishing is woven, in the dark green background a similar scene in silhouette.

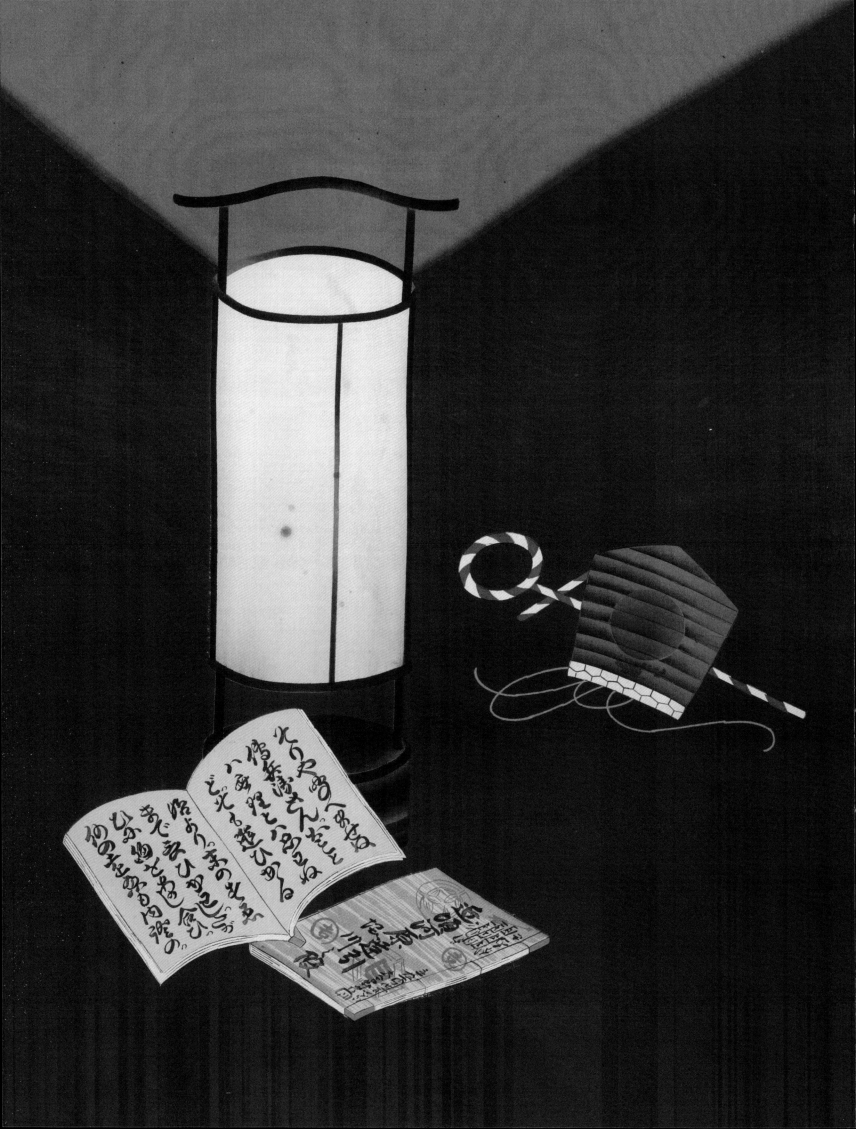

Men's Under-Kimono
Private Images

Like in most types of kimono, the emphasis of the decoration on men's under-kimono (*nagajuban*) lay on the back. Any front patterns were merely extensions of the design on the backside.

At first glance, the subjects seem very nostalgic in the majority of cases, full of longing for the bygone Tokugawa era with its views, its stories and its art. However, on closer examination several apparently traditional images in fact represent contemporary topics. The kimono with the large *mimasu* crest ('three nesting rice measures') and the lobster was made on the occasion of the name change of the kabuki actor Ichikawa Danjurō XI in May 1940 (cat. 77), and the half-size portraits of kabuki actors on another kimono were done in the Shin Hanga or 'new print' style, which had been developed since 1915 (cat. 76). Dating from the 1930s are the kimono with images of the imminent war with China (cat. 78, 79).

Nearly all designs have been done in stencil printing with the use of a mixture of dyes with rice paste (*kata-yūzen*). Colours are subdued. The freehand painted design of a half-naked lady taking a bath (cat. 74) is exceptional.

The silk is always plain weave; figured silk or damask weave was not for men. Occasionally, under-kimono were made of raw silk (*tsumugi*) and one half-length *nagajuban* in this collection is partly made of cotton (cat. 71, 75).

Nagajuban were covered by plain dark outer kimono. Therefore none of the designs would ever be seen in public, not even in restaurants or theatres. The only occasions where the textile secrets may sometimes have been revealed were the private gatherings with friends in small parlours (*zashiki*). In artful expressions, which could include song and dance, one could make a personal statement, be it on a favourite kabuki actor or on a political topic. In such an ambiance the designs on *haori* linings and under-kimono may have played a role.[1]

[1] Kashiwagi 2005: 171-81.

66. Dragons in clouds
Man's *nagajuban* (no crests)
Outside: grey and white crepe silk
(*chirimen*) with stencil-printed
decoration, direct-dye (*kata-yūzen*)
Lining: the upper part of the body is
lined with white silk
121 × 128 cm
1900–20

The body has a dynamic all-over
decoration with dragons in the clouds,
whereas the sleeves are plain. Although
the dragonheads were painted with the
use of stencils, the clouds are partially
done in freehand painting.

67. Shōki and *oni*

Man's *nagajuban* (no crests)
Outside: plain weave silk with
stencil-printed, direct-dye decoration
(*kata-yūzen*)
Lining: cream lining of the body
125 × 124 cm
1920–40

Oni or 'devils' are mischievous imps who used to haunt households. They are of human form, but have two horns on their heads, three fingers tipped with claws and only wear loincloths. For the sake of peace and happiness *oni* must be exorcised at New Year by throwing beans. Like on this under-kimono their devilry is mostly depicted as being of a humorous kind: here they are creeping into the seams to tease the wearer. Who could be the supposed wearer of this under-kimono? The fact that the *oni* are teasing him and that he is carrying a large iron rod (*kanabō*) may indicate that he is Shōki, the mythical Chinese hero, who had resolved to devote himself to expel all devils from the empire. In Japan, however, he is usually depicted rather as the victim of the nasty *oni* than as their hunter. At the upper end of the club, one can even perceive the mocking mirror image of an *oni*'s face. The two large overlapping squares of the *manryoku mon* represent 'thousand-fold power'.

Man's *nagajuban* (no crests)
Outside: plain weave silk with stencil-printed, direct-dye decoration (*kata-yūzen*)
Lining: brown silk
132 × 129 cm
1920–40

A peasant's home on the bank of a lake surrounded by wooded mountains is the subject of the folding screen. Three young people are making music. A youngster seated on a lacquer chest is beating his shoulder drum, another young man, seated on the floor, is playing the *shamisen*, and an elegant young lady in kimono with a design of banana leaves also plays the *shamisen*. A smoking set lies on the floor.
In the seventeenth century such cheerful scenes were often depicted on screens, but these were painted in bright pigments on a gold leaf ground instead of in monochromes. However, subdued colours were favoured for menswear, even in the extrovert Taishō period.

69. Oshun and Denbei

Man's *nagajuban* (no crests)
Outside: plain weave silk with
stencil-printed, direct-dye decoration
(*kata-yūzen*)
Lining: cream silk
130 × 129 cm
1920–40

In the light of a lamp, the following
scene can be observed. A man and a
lady are walking hand-in-hand: they
must be lovers. The lady is biting on
her headscarf, indicating that she is in
distress. Her kimono is decorated with
wild carnations, symbols of fidelity. The
man is wearing a straw hat, he doesn't
want to be recognised. In the distance
the Kiyomizu temple in Higashiyama,
and therefore we know that the setting
is Kyoto. Next to the lamp, two
attributes of the Monkey Showman
(*sarumawashi*) have been laid on the
floor, and also two books.
All these elements indicate that the
scene illustrates the tragic story of
Denbei and Oshun. Denbei was a
Kyoto merchant who fell passionately
in love with the courtesan Oshun from
the Gion district of Higashiyama. He
decided to raise money and redeem her.
His rival was an evil samurai,
Yokobuchi Kanzaemon, whom he
eventually killed. The lovers then fled
to take their own lives in a *shinjū*
('oneness of hearts', meaning a double
love suicide) despite the efforts of
Oshun's brother Yoshirō to prevent it.
As a compassionate brother and
professional monkey trainer, all he
could do was to have his monkey
perform an entertaining dance as the
two lovers drank their *sake* from the
'marriage' cups. Yoshirō then had to
allow his sister Oshun and Denbei to
make their final journey: the scene
shown in the lamplight.[1]
The title of the book on the floor reads
Chikagoro kawara no tatehiki, a story
and play popularly known as 'Oshun-
Denbei'.

[1] The Oshun-Denbei story was found
on the website OsakaPrints.com

70. Under the bridge
Man's *nagajuban* (no crests)
Outside: plain weave silk with
stencil-printed, direct-dye decoration
(*kata-yūzen*)
Lining: off-white cotton
131 × 130 cm
1920–40

On the front of this under-kimono,
a large curve separates the black field
from the brown areas beneath. On the
backside the curve gets a meaning.
As the result of the addition of a huge
pillar, the curve is transformed into the
silhouette of a high bridge under which
two small boats are depicted. It seems
to be twilight. In the light of the setting
sun, the snow-covered top of Mount
Fuji and two white sails can still be
clearly seen in the distance.

71. *Inrō* and *netsuke*
Man's *nagajuban* (no crests)
Outside: green raw silk (*tsumugi*); plain
weave with stencil-printed, direct-dye
decoration (*kata-yūzen*)
Inside: green rayon (*jinken*)
127 × 126 cm
1920–40

During the Edo period lacquered
medicine containers (*inrō*) were the
most highly esteemed accessories for a
man's dress, hung from the narrow *obi*
(see 115). With a silk cord the *inrō* was
attached to a miniature carving of ivory
or wood: the *netsuke*. The *netsuke* was
slipped under the *obi* and served as a
toggle to prevent the *inrō* from falling.
In the beginning of the twentieth
century, *inrō* were rarely worn any
longer. This under-kimono must have
been worn by a nostalgic gentleman.
On the green raw silk, ten different *inrō*
are depicted, in several cases forming
meaningful ensembles with their
matching *netsuke*: waves and plover,
horse and gourd, crane and turtle,
lobster and shell.

72. Ukiyoe couple

Man's *nagajuban* (no crests)
Outside: plain weave silk with
stencil-printed, direct-dye decoration
(*kata-yūzen*)
Lining: off-white silk
133 × 132 cm
1920–40

Sometimes one comes across men's
haori or *nagajuban* with designs after
Ukiyoe woodblock prints. Although the
decoration of this under-kimono is not
an exact copy of the woodblock print,
it is likely to be based on the famous
print *Lovers in the Snow: the Crow
and the Heron* by Suzuki Harunobu
(1725?–70) (see illustration).

The second part of the title is derived
from the fact that on the original print
the young man is dressed in black (like
a crow) and the young lady in white
(like a heron).
On the kimono both figures might be
thought to be female, but the fact that
the figure on the left has much shorter
sleeves and that the pair are watching a
couple of mandarin ducks (an emblem
of conjugal love) strongly suggest that
they are a man and a woman, and
a couple as well. Like on Harunobu's
print they are walking in the snow,
but here beside a pond or brook.
The willow tree and the dwarf bamboo
are covered with snow. The lower
end of the kimono shows hundreds
of characters signifying good luck.

Woodblock-print *Lovers in the Snow*
by Suzuki Harunobu (1725?–70), from
Henri L. Joly & Kumasaku Tomita,
Japanese Art & Handicraft, 1916, Plate
XV, no. 9.

73. Dragon rising to heaven
Man's *nagajuban* (no crests)
Outside: plain weave silk with stencil-printed, direct-dye decoration (*kata-yūzen*), gold foil application and extensive splashing (*nori-koboshi*)
Inscription: 'dragon rising towards heaven' (*ryū shōten*); 'Shiun *ga*' and seal 'Shiun'
Lining: white silk

132 × 129 cm
1920–40

The design of this under-kimono looks like a painting, but is actually done in very skilled stencil work. Only the splashed white paint lies on top of the silk, the other colours have been absorbed into the fibres.
The model was a painting by the Kyoto painter Shiun, who was active in the period 1910–40. In this case also the title has been inscribed next to the signature.
The under-kimono shows three broad bands of a brown grid pattern (*hakezome*).

74. Seated lady taking a bath

Man's *nagajuban* (no crests)
Outside: plain weave silk with freehand painted decoration (*tegaki-yūzen*) and shell powder pigment (*gofun*)
Inscription: 'Eisen *e*'
Lining: cream silk
140 × 137 cm
1930–50

The design after a painting by Eisen has been executed in the freehand, so-called direct *yūzen* technique without paste-resist outlining. The white skin of the lady has been painted with a thick layer of shell powder, as are the white stripes of her kimono. In the background a half-lowered bamboo blind can be observed, which enhances the private atmosphere of the depiction. Such mildly erotic pictures are often referred to as *abuna-e* or *risqué* images.

75. The horseracing season of 1926–1927
Man's *hanjuban* (no crests)
Outside: the body made of cotton, the sleeves of silk; stencil-printed, direct-dye method (*kata-yūzen*)
Lining: the body has white cotton lining, the sleeves an ivory silk lining
127 × 87 cm
1926–27

This half-length under-kimono has sleeves with betting tickets of 20 yen for the racing season from autumn 1926 to spring 1927. Between the tickets, racing horses are depicted. The bodice shows numerous coins, symbolising the money the owner of the jacket obviously hoped to win. Western-style horse races were first organised by foreign residents of Yokohama in 1862; betting tickets were first sold in 1888. Betting was prohibited by the government in 1906, but in 1923 eleven horse racing clubs were licensed to organise races and sell betting tickets again. One wonders whether KRC stands for Kyoto Racing Club.

76. Kabuki actors
Man's *nagajuban* (no crests)
Outside: crepe silk (*chirimen*) with
stencil-printed, direct-dye decoration
(*kata-yūzen*)
Lining: white silk lining of the body
130 × 129 cm
1920–40

On the backside of this under-kimono, two half-size portraits are depicted of a young actor with a dotted headscarf and an older actor wearing a scarf with pine needle decoration. Kabuki connoisseurs recognise them as 'Scarfaced Yosa' (note the red scars on his chest) and 'Yasu the Bat', partners in crime in the kabuki play *The Love Affair of Otomi and Scarfaced Yosaburō*. The texts on the paper strips within the rectangles behind the actors may represent the visiting cards of their sponsors. Also on the back, three black crests of the kabuki actors Nakamura Shikan, Morita Kanya and Ichikawa Sadanji. On the front of the right sleeve two additional crests: the triple rice measures with the '*sa*' character of Ichikawa Sadanji and the other one of Jitsukawa Ensaburō.

**77. The kabuki actor Ichikawa
Dajurō changes his name**
Man's *nagajuban* (no crests)
Outside: crepe silk (*chirimen*) with
stencil-printed, direct-dye decoration
(*kata-yūzen*) and scattered gold leaf
Lining: white silk lining of the body
130 × 129 cm
1940

Like the *haori* for the birth of Emperor
Akihito, this *nagajuban* is an occasional
garment. Thanks to the large triple
square crests on both sides, it is not
difficult to guess that this under-
kimono has something to do with
Ichikawa Danjurō, but which
generation of this famous family of
kabuki actors and what is the meaning
of the lobster?
A print designed by Katsukawa
Shunshō (1726–92) published in 1772
shows Ichikawa Danjurō IV in the
shibaraku role with enormous nesting
rice measures (*mimasu-mon*) on his
sleeves, and two large lobsters (*ebi*)
superimposed (see illustration).
This print was issued to commemorate
the actor's change of name to Ebizō II
that year.
The kimono must have been
manufactured for a similar occasion,
since the lobster is changing its shell,
indicating that it is about to enter a
new stage in its life. The Ichikawa
genealogy reveals that Ichikawa
Danjurō XI changed his name to
Ebizō IX in May 1940. Since the name
Ebizō VIII was adopted in 1881 and
the name Ebizō X in 1969 (both
unlikely dates for the kimono), it can
safely be concluded that this under-
kimono was made on the occasion of
the name change in 1940, and for his
fans, of course.
At the lower end of the black field
numerous names of other kabuki actors
are listed: the Kataokas, the Ichimarus,
the Ichikawas, the Arashis, etc.

Woodblock-print: *Ichikawa Danjurō
VII in the* shibaraku *role*, by Katsukawa
Shunshō (1726–92).
Private collection (Netherlands).

78. The Mukden and Shanghai Incidents

Man's *nagajuban* (no crests)
Outside: plain weave silk with stencil-printed, direct-dye decoration (*kata-yūzen*)
Lining: blue and white silk
136 × 128 cm
1932

The Treaty of Portsmouth, which ended the Russo-Japanese War of 1904–1905, provided for the transfer of Russian interests in Manchuria to Japan, including the jurisdictional and administrative power of the railway zone. From 1907 onwards, the South Manchurian Railway (Mantetsu) dominated economic life in Manchuria. Circles in the Japanese army, however, wanted to expand its power in the region further. The 1931 Mukden Incident provided the radicals in the army with the pretext for a campaign to conquer Manchuria during the winter of 1931–32, and establish the puppet-state Manchukuo. This is the remarkable topic of this kimono.
One pair of rectangles depicts the shooting of an SMR-train by Chinese soldiers, and also the railway network around Mukden (now Shenyang).
The other pair of rectangles shows the 1932 Shanghai Incident – including a map of the area – with a silhouette of the Bunt and Japanese warships skirmishing with Chinese armed forces. This incident led Western countries, who had their own interests in Shanghai, to condemn the Japanese intervention.
Ten days after the signing of the truce in May 1932, Prime Minister Inukai Tsuyoshi, who had tried to withhold or at least postpone the recognition of Manchukuo, was assassinated by right-wing ultranationalists, so putting party politics in pre-war Japan to an end and starting further escalation to war.
The background of the under-kimono shows Japanese troops marching in the snow during the Manchurian campaign of 1931–32.

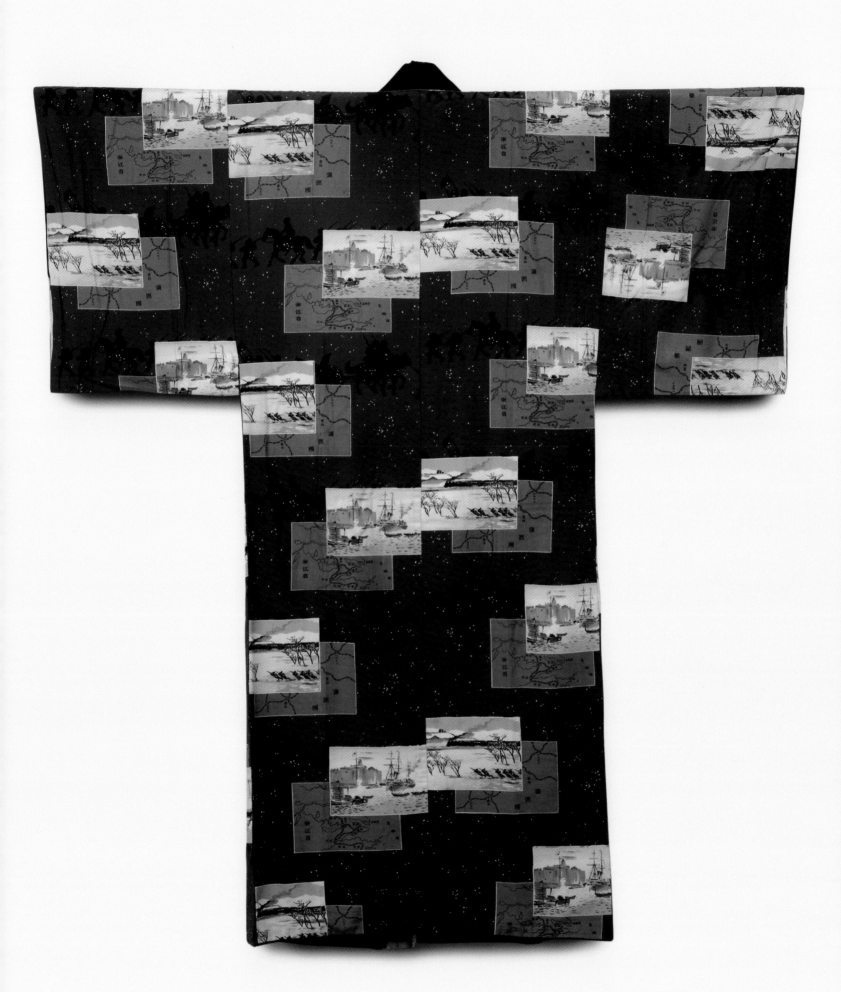

79. Skulls

Man's *nagajuban* (no crests)
Outside: plain weave silk with
stencil-printed, direct-dye decoration
(*kata-yūzen*)
Lining: orange-brown silk
132 × 132 cm
1930–40

White skulls and black texts of poems
are scattered over the surface of this
olive-green under-kimono. The message
seems to convey that the wearer is
prepared to die for the sake of his
country: "I will go, even if I may die
and my corpse be exposed to the
elements".

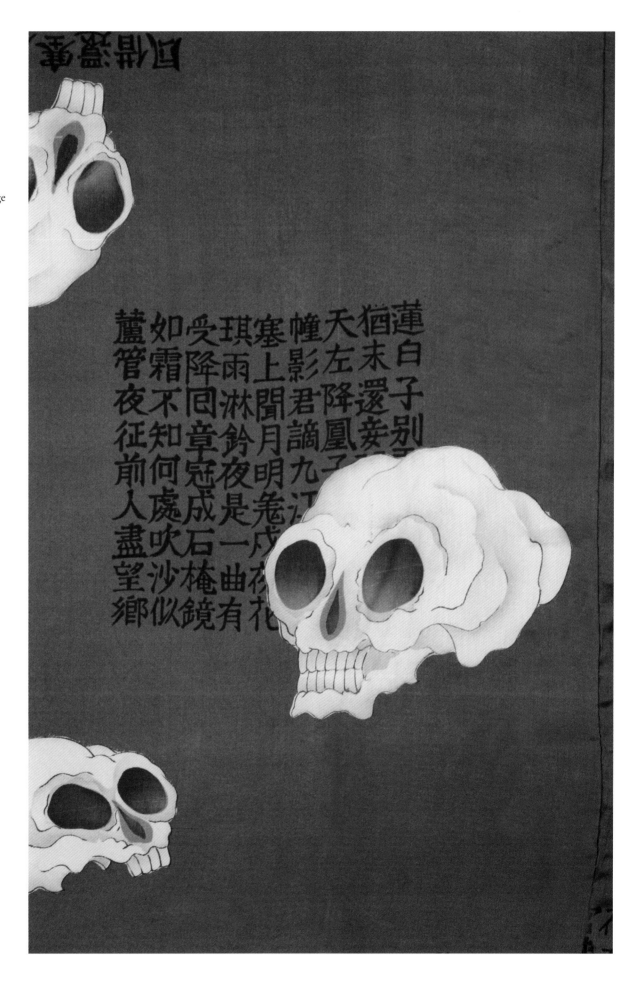

Children's Kimono
Contrasting Expectations

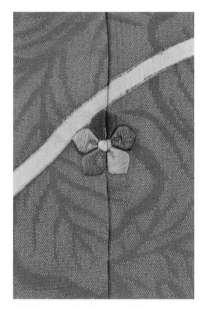

39. Three embroidery techniques: (a) flat stitch embroidery or *hira-nui* (up), (b) French-knot embroidery or *sagara-nui* and (c) alternating long and short stitches of *sashi-nui* (bottom)

From the time of birth onwards, contrasting future expectations played a major role in the upbringing of girls and boys, and these were reflected in their respective kimono (cat. 80–86, and cat. 87–98). Girls' kimono came in three varieties: sweet, sweeter and sweetest (fig. 38). Flowers and cranes in vibrant colours were the most frequent motifs.

Damask woven silk fabric was often used with *yūzen* decorations (the classical *tsutsugaki* variant) and additional embroidery. Two types of embroidery were common: flat-stitch (*hira-nui*) (fig. 39a), which produced a rich sheen and was therefore suitable for placing accents, and French knot embroidery (*sagara-nui*) (fig. 39b), which produced granules in the hearts of flowers and on the red heads of cranes. The embroidery of larger areas was done in alternating short and long stitches (*sashi-nui*) (fig. 39c).

Boys' kimono were typically decorated with symbols of strength and perseverance, such as powerful animals or warriors. Even when toys were depicted, these were often of a martial kind. Compared to girl's kimono, the colours were more restrained (fig. 40).

Damask silks were not used for boys' garments, the fabric had to be plain weave. Decorations were executed in either *tsutsugaki yūzen* (rice paste outlining) or *tegaki-yūzen* (freehand painted).

Miyamairi kimono constitute a large category. Such garments were meant for the first visit of a newborn infant to the local Shinto shrine, on the 20th, 30th, 50th up to the 100th day after birth to have it recognised by the local tutelary deity as a member of the Shinto community. In fact the infant was still too small to wear the kimono, but was rather wrapped in it when being carried by one of the grandmothers (fig. 41). The two straps were tied around the grandmother's neck. Family members congratulated the child by tucking paper money between the straps. Where the left strap is attached to the lapel, a geometrical stitching (*semamori*) can often be observed, which served as a charm and appeared in all kinds of variants (fig. 42).

Opposite
38. Little girl in opulent kimono (1920s). Ikjeld.com

40. Boy in blue festive jacket watching the preparation of a candy floss. Postcard, author's collection

41. Reproduction of a woodblock print showing how the grandmother carries a baby in *miyamairi* kimono to the Shinto shrine. Postcard, author's collection

42. *Semamori* stitches on infants' *miyamairi* kimono were meant as charms against evil

(6) They going to a shinto shrine.

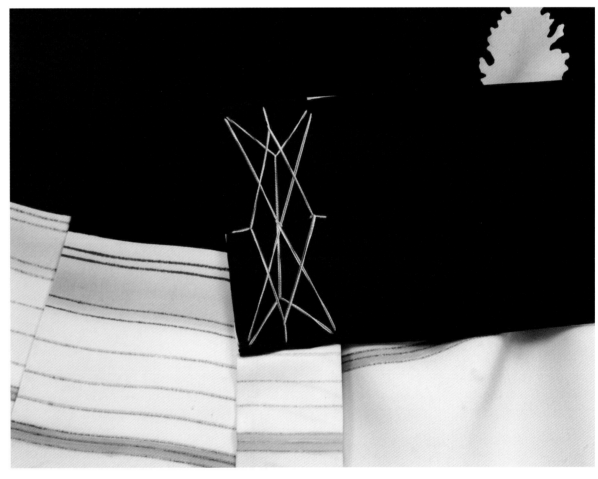

80. *Koto*, curtains and chrysanthemums

Girl's *furisode* with padded hem
(five crests)
Outside: yellow silk, damask weave
(*rinzu*); hand-painted with rice-paste
resist outlining (*yūzen*), *sagara-nui*
embroidery and couched gold
Crest: melon (*mokko*)
Lining: red silk
114 × 108 cm
1890–1910

The lower part of the backside panels
feature a *koto* (horizontal string
instrument) half inside its cover and
surrounded by peonies and
chrysanthemums. In addition, an open
fan is decorated with a flowering plum
on the waterside, and its cover is in
wood imitation (*mokume*). On the
front panels and both sides of the
sleeves parts of stands with silk curtains
(*kichō*) are visible, again surrounded by
peonies and chrysanthemums. In Heian
times an aristocratic lady would receive
gentlemen callers concealed by such
'screens of state'; only her long sleeves
would sometimes protrude outside the
curtains. This remarkably light-weight
furisode shows the elegance of those
screens well: the patterns of all hangings
are different.
Several outlines and other details are
accentuated by double gold threads
attached to the surface by minute red
stitches. The hearts of the flowers are all
done in delicate yellow French knot
embroidery. The silk itself is patterned
with tiny paulownia motifs.

81. Flowering plants

Girl's *miyamairi* kimono (five crests)
Outside: purple silk, damask weave
(*rinzu*); hand-painted with rice-paste
resist outlining (*yūzen*), and embroidery
Crest: melon (*mokko*)
Lining: red silk
99 × 87 cm
1900–20

During the Tokugawa period, clothing
coloured deep purple was reserved for
the ruling class. Therefore this colour
became popular during the subsequent
Meiji era as soon as the restrictions had
been lifted. The pigment had become
more readily available as the chemical
dye 'Perkins purple' since 1856, and it
was admired because the colour was
even more brilliant than the purple
plant dyes from the past.
This *miyamairi* kimono, in which a
baby girl was wrapped during her first
visit to the Shinto shrine, is decorated
with a profusion of flowers:
chrysanthemums, peonies, hibiscus,
Chinese bells and maiden's flowers.
Even the straps on the front are
adorned with flowers, and the silk itself
is figured with chrysanthemums,
paulownia and bamboo.
Many leaves and petals show fine
grading of the colours, and several
kinds of embroidery were employed in
the hearts of the flowers. At the outer
edges of the long sleeves, the bright red
lining has been sewn in such a way as
to come out and contrast with the deep
purple. The basting stitches of the
sleeves are still present.

Girl's kimono (no crests)
Outside: black silk; damask weave
(*rinzu*) with stencil-printed, direct-dye
decoration (*kata-yūzen*), and
embroidered details
Lining: pale pink cotton
109 × 103 cm
1920–40

Flowering camellia twigs trail the length
of the kimono, their strong colours
contrasting with the formal cloud
patterns in the black background. In
the upper section behind several flower
petals stand out as the result of yellow
embroidery. In women's kimono one
often finds embroidery at the lower end
of the garment, but in the case of a
little girl such additions would have
been hardly visible.
The shoulders were tucked to adapt to
the girl's size.

83. Wild carnations

Girl's *miyamairi furisode* (five crests)
Outside: violet gauze crepe silk
(*ro chirimen*); hand-painted with
rice-paste resist outlining (*yūzen*),
embroidery and couched gold
Lining: shoulder and lower body lining
of white sheer crepe silk (*ro chirimen*)
Crest: bamboo (*take*)
Unlined
91 × 82 cm
1920–40

This transparent violet *furisode* shows
several kinds of wild carnations
(*nadeshiko*) by a stream. Also the straps
are decorated with flowers. *Nadeshiko*
is one of the seven autumn herbs
(*aki no nanakusa*), and considered
a symbol of fidelity.
The large motifs have been sparingly
enlivened by embroidery and gold
couched threads. The pink carnations
show square patterns on their petals
as if they were done in the *shibori*
tie-dye technique. Such simulations
were already common during the
Tokugawa period.
Ro chirimen is a rare combination
of weaving techniques. *Ro* gauze fabric
would be preferred during the hot
summer months; the *chirimen* weaving,
which makes use of 'overspun' twisted
threads, gives this kimono a pleasant
feel.

84. Cranes flying over the waves
Girl's *miyamairi* kimono (no crests)
Outside: damask-woven silk (*rinzu*);
hand-painted with rice-paste resist
outlining (*yūzen*), embroidery, gold
and silver leaf application, coached
gold and silver
Lining: red silk
104 × 87 cm
1920–40

The orange, yellow and blue horizontal
fields seem to represent water, land and
sky. Vividly rendered cranes are flying
in the air, their sizes somewhat
increasing towards the lower hem, their
wings in graded orange, yellow, blue
and purple with additions of
embroidery in white silk. The red spots
on the heads of the cranes have *sagara-
nui* or French knot embroidery in red

and gold, some of their black tails are
outlined with gold couched threads.
Also the crests of the waves and the
splashing foam are done in embroidery.
Squares of gold and silver leaf have
been applied to the blue parts of
the kimono, just as can sometimes
be seen on old calligraphy hand-scrolls.
The fabric itself has faint cloud
patterns.

85. Traditional textile patterns
Girl's *miyamairi* kimono (no crests)
Outside: pink crepe silk (*chirimen*)
with stencil-printed, direct-dye
decoration (*kata-yūzen*)
Lining: shoulder lining of red silk with
tie-dye decoration (*shibori*)
78 × 70 cm
1920–40

This garment is mainly dyed pink and
red. Various traditional textile patterns
have been arranged over the surface,
divided by bold zigzag lines. The very
small size would fit the small girl much
better than the oversized *miyamairi*
kimono on the preceding pages.

86. Spinning tops

Girl's *miyamairi* kimono (no crests)
Outside: blue crepe silk (*chirimen*) with
stencil-printed, direct-dye decoration
(*kata-yūzen*)
Lining: pink crepe silk (*chirimen*)
82 × 81 cm
1920–40

Against a dark-blue and pale-blue
chequered background, spinning tops
of various sizes are placed in bright
colours. These geometrical forms make
a much more modern impression than
most floral motifs of *miyamairi*
kimono; moreover the design of tops
is closer to the child's world.
In this case the straps are of plain pink
crepe silk, as is the lining.

87. Leaping carp

Boy's *miyamairi* kimono (five crests)
Outside: black silk; plain weave
with hand-painted ink and colours
(*tegeki-yūzen*), embroidery, couched
gold and gold leaf application
Crest: star (*hoshi*)
Lining: white silk
98 × 88 cm
1920–40

The carp was a common motif on boys'
kimono as the symbol of perseverance
and the will to win, qualities parents
wished their sons to acquire. The carp
battles against the stream and
overcomes rapids and waterfalls. In
ancient China, these fish were believed
to become dragons once they had
mastered the Dragon Gate rapids in the
Yellow River.
The decoration seems to be painted
freehand, whereas the white foam of the
waves seems to be splashed onto the
textile. The eyes of both carp have been
embroidered, whereas the fins are
outlined with couched gold. Gold foil
application can be seen on the leaves of
the small bamboo plants.

88. White eagle
Boy's *miyamairi* kimono (five crests)
Outside: black silk, plain weave;
hand-painted with rice paste resist
outlining (*yūzen*), gold and silver leaf
application, and couched silver
Crest: pine (*matsu*)
Lining: cream silk
89 × 85 cm
1920–40

A giant white eagle with outspread
wings adorns this boy's ceremonial
kimono. Of course, it is another
emblem of strength and power.
Silver and gold foil application
and couched silver provide the scene
with glitter in the changing light.
Interestingly, the extreme ends of the
wings are depicted twice: not only
on the sleeves, but also on the front
of the body.

89. Chinese lion on gold screen
Boy's *miyamairi* kimono (five crests)
Outside: black plain weave silk
with hand-painted ink and colours
(*tegaki-yūzen*), embroidery and
extensive application of gold foil
Crest: paulownia (*kiri*)
Lining: cream silk
100 × 84 cm
1920–40

The mythical *karashishi* or Chinese lion
was believed to be so powerful that it
was able to run a distance of 500 miles
in a single night. The animal was also
considered a guardian against evil. On
New Year's Day, *Shishimai* dancers
exorcised all the evil of the previous
year.
The background of this kimono has
numerous squares of gold leaf,
suggesting a screen or sliding door.
The screen shows a painting of a *shishi*
jumping from rock to rock over the
rapids. The curling mane is enlivened
by gold foil, whereas the eyes, the claws
of the forepaws and the single tooth
have applications of couched gold.
Family members and friends, who
accompanied the young boy on his first
visit to the Shinto shrine would attach
bank notes as presents to the loose
threads on the back.

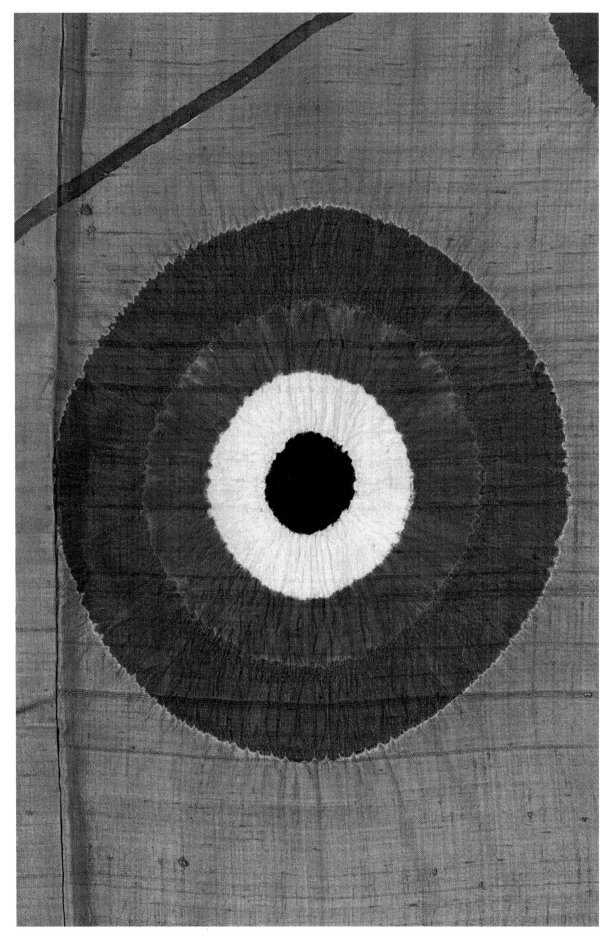

90. Arrow and targets
Boy's *miyamairi* kimono (five crests)
Outside: hand-woven plain weave
of hand-spun raw silk (*tsumugi*)
with tie-dye decoration (*shibori*)
Crest: paulownia (*kiri*)
Lining: white plain-weave silk
98 × 81 cm
1920–40

This kimono was made by hand from
threads to finished garment. The fine
quality probably indicates that it was
custom ordered. The five crests were
already incorporated during the dyeing
process and not added after the
completion of the kimono.
The motifs were created by stitching
the outlines and drawing up the threads
before dyeing. The variously coloured
rings could be created in several stages
of capping parts of the motifs with
impermeable material, and the same
number of dye baths. Although this
technique is also called *shibori*, it
concerns another variant than the one
discussed in cat. 8. In fact, *shibori*
involves a whole range of tie-and-dye
methods.

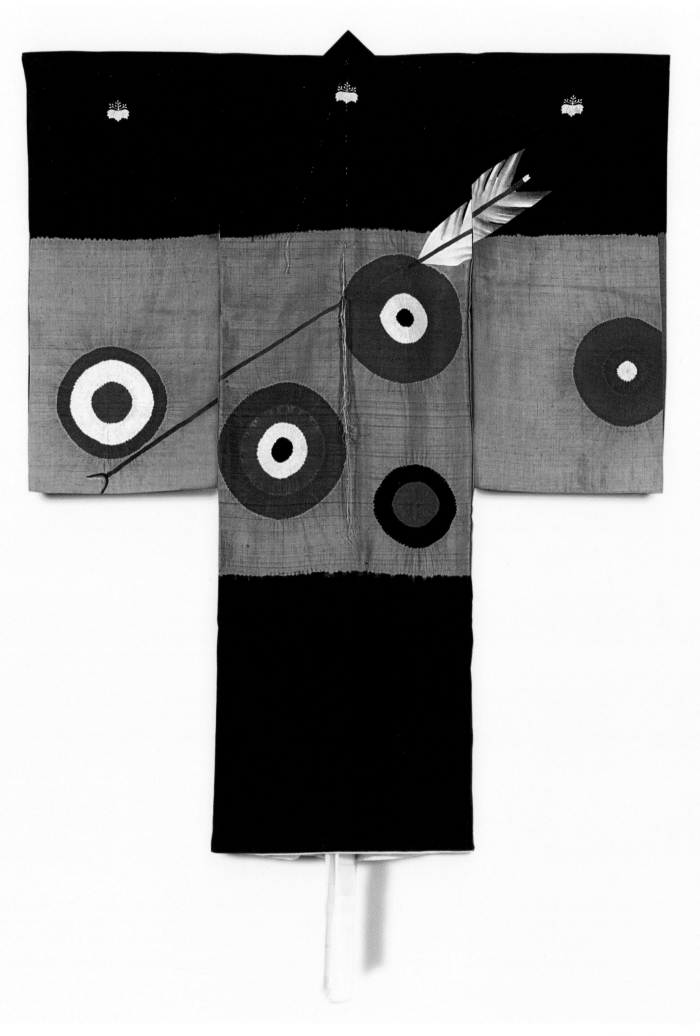

**91. Samurai on horseback
and Mount Fuji**
Boy's *miyamairi* kimono (five crests)
Outside: black plain weave silk with
hand-painted ink and colours (*tegaki-
yūzen*), embroidery, application of gold
foil, and couched silver and gold
thread.
Crest: wood sorrel (*katabami*)
Lining: white silk in the body; double
lining of the sleeves with an additional
layer of pale damask-woven silk (*rinzu*)
103 × 85 cm
1920–40

Apart from powerful animals, samurai
were another popular theme for boys'
ceremonial kimono. In this case it
concerns a samurai in full armour on
horseback. He is standing on the beach
with a view of distant Mount Fuji over
the breaking waves. Several ships with
the same banner as the warrior carries
lie at anchor. The scene suggests an
episode from a heroic story.
An attractive contrast has been attained
between the meticulously drawn horse
and samurai with the slightly blurred
outlines of the green pines and the dark
rocks. The waves were done in rather
wet brush strokes, resulting in a soft
effect.

92. Samurai on horseback with attendant

Boy's *miyamairi* kimono (five crests)
Outside: black plain weave silk with hand-painted ink and colours (*yūzen*); basting stitches on the sleeves
Crest: mesh (*meyui*)
Lining: white silk in the body; double lining of the sleeves with an additional layer of pale yellow damask-woven silk (*rinzu*). Separate plain white silk under-kimono
109 × 86 cm
1920–40

Although the subject matter is related to the previous kimono, it has been rendered all-over in precision painting without any blurring or tonality of hues, apart from some grading in the treetops and roofs of the buildings. Most boys' *miyamairi* kimono – and this example is no exception – were decorated on the middle part of the body and the lower two-thirds of the sleeves. Often interesting solutions were found to prevent just a simple straight demarcation line to the black fields. In this kimono, the designer created fascinating silhouettes of roofs and treetops in black at the lower demarcation, which act as the counterpart to the roofs and treetops above the wall at the upper demarcation.

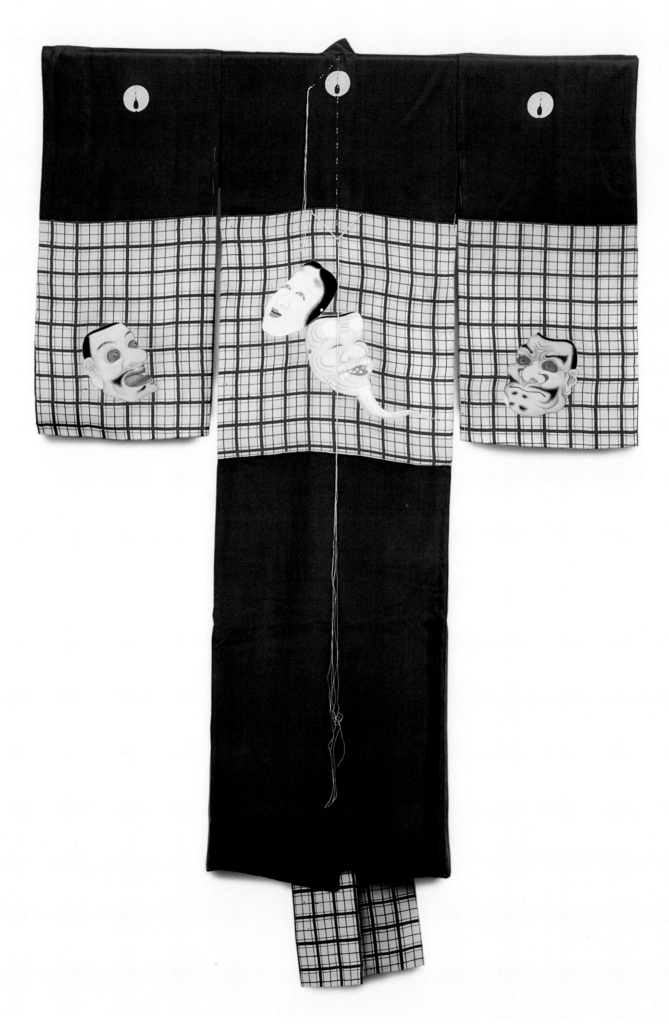

93. Nine *nō* masks

Boy's *miyamairi* kimono (five crests)
Outside: blue silk, plain weave; hand-painted with rice-paste resist outlining (*yūzen*) and application of gold leaf
Crest: apricot shoots (*gyoyo*)
Lining: white silk
Brand tag: H.INOUE . DAIMARU . KYOTO
117 × 88 cm
1920–40

Nine *nō* masks are placed against a checked background, one of these is a boy's mask. Each mask is rendered realistically with very fine grading of colours and detailed painting of the hair. The bulging eyes of two masks have an application of gold foil to imitate the metal inlays of the real wooden *nō* masks, which were used as models. Uncommon is the brand tag with the inscription 'H. Inoue' in both Japanese characters and Roman script, and in addition the name of the department store Daimaru. Like the department stores Takashimaya, Mitsukoshi and Isetan, Daimaru started as a kimono retail shop.

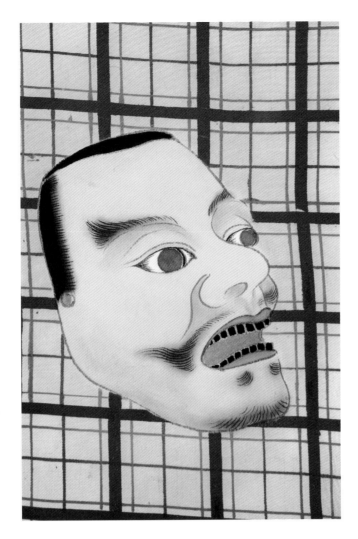

94. Transportation

Boy's padded *miyamairi* kimono
(no crests)
Outside: blue plain weave silk;
stencil-printed, direct-dye method
(*kata-yūzen*)
Lining: white silk
84 × 79 cm
1920–40

Five different motifs are shown inside
circles. All are related to transportation:
a steam locomotive, a zeppelin and
airplanes, a cable lift, probably a racing
track, and boats (albeit in *origami* like
the folded cranes above them). The
architecture of some of the buildings
suggests that not all the scenes are
located in Japan.

95. Boy's toys

Set of a boy's *miyamairi* kimono and *haori*

95a. Boy's kimono (five crests), part of a set
Outside: black *habutae* silk; hand-painted with rice-paste resist outlining (*yūzen*) on the ribbons
Crest: oak (*kashiwa*)
Lining: white silk
112 × 87 cm
1920–40

Only the straps, which were tied around the mother's or grandmother's neck while carrying the baby to the Shinto shrine, are decorated. Several kinds of toys have been artistically painted in attractive colours.
This kimono was part of an ensemble with the *haori* on the next pages.

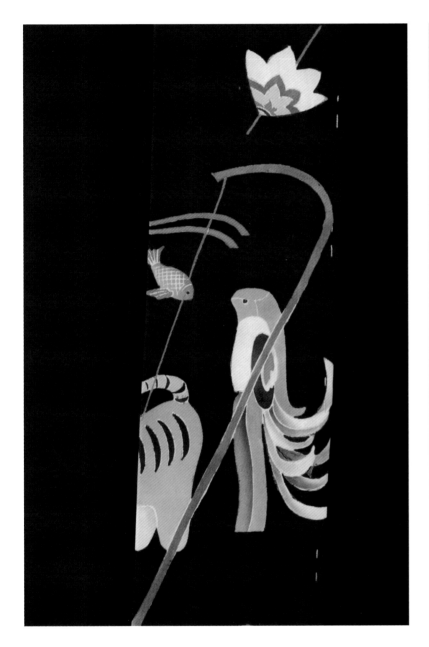

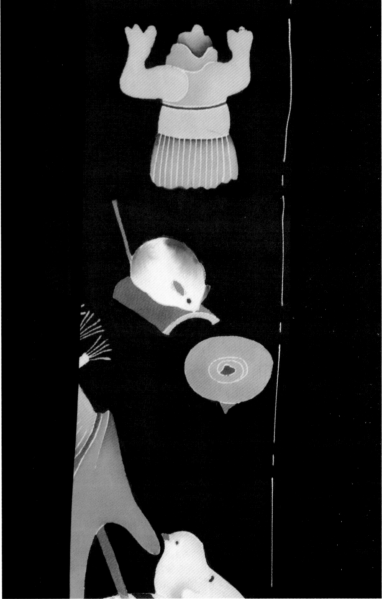

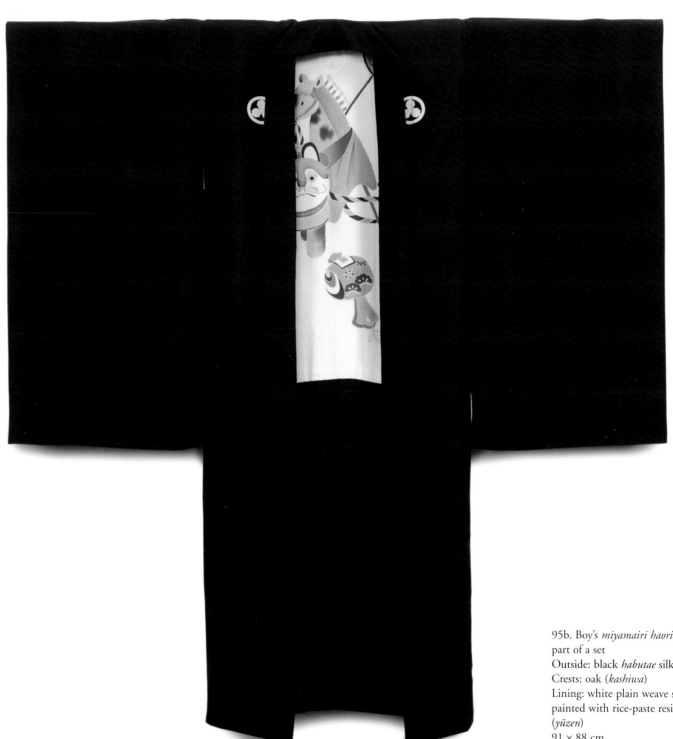

95b. Boy's *miyamairi haori* (five crests), part of a set
Outside: black *habutae* silk
Crests: oak (*kashiwa*)
Lining: white plain weave silk; hand-painted with rice-paste resist outlining (*yūzen*)
91 × 88 cm
1920–40

Many kinds of toys, rendered in fine painting, are scattered over the lining of this jacket. In between, somewhat smaller good luck symbols – such as flaming pearls and Daikoku's hammer – can be seen. The purpose of the boy's first visit to the Shinto shrine was to promote his good fortune and good health in future life. An ensemble like this one must have been very expensive, only affordable to a wealthy family.

96. Gramophone records

Boy's kimono (no crests)
Outside: plain weave wool; printed
Inside: plain weave cotton
78 × 80 cm
1920–40

Broad blue bands alternate with chequered bands. Superimposed on this pattern, black gramophone records and record sleeves interrupt the regularity of rectangles and squares. They are *kodomo* or children's records. A small dog is watching a boy, who is dancing on a barrel. A pair of birds is quietly perched on the gramophone records, as if this were the most normal thing to happen.

97. The coronation of King George VI
Boy's kimono (no crests)
Outside: plain weave rayon (*jinken*);
stencil-printed, direct-dye method
(*kata-yūzen*)
Inside: plain weave cotton
77 × 76 cm
1937

The boy waving the Rising Sun flag
and the Union Jack makes clear that
the main topic of this small garment is
about Japanese-British relations.
The green background of the Union
Jack can be understood by the fact that
green and blue are considered in Japan
as two tints of the colour *aoi*.
Mount Fuji obviously symbolises Japan.
The crown appears to be the Imperial
State Crown of Great Britain,
recognisable by the Maltese cross on
the top, the Black Prince's Ruby
(actually a spinel) in the centre-front
and the large Cullinan II diamond or
'lesser Star of Africa' in the front rim
(this was the second largest diamond
cut from the huge stone found in South
Africa by Frederick Wells in 1905;
the Cullinan I diamond or 'Star of
Africa' is set to the Royal Sceptre, but
not visible on this textile).[1]
Although the connection with the
main topic remains obscure, the
airplane helps date this kimono.
The letters KNILM on the wings
must be the abbreviation of Koninklijke
Nederlandsch-Indische
Luchtvaartmaatschappij (Royal
Netherlands Indies' Airways),
a company founded in 1928
and dissolved in 1947. One of their
favourite planes was the Fokker
VIIb-3m, fitted with three engines.
This plane seems to be depicted
on the boy's kimono.
Since the plane dates from before
World War II, and since KNILM was
dissolved in 1947, it is unlikely that the
Imperial State Crown refers to the
coronation of Queen Elizabeth in 1953,
but rather to the coronation of King
George VI in 1937. On the latter
occasion, a record flight – sponsored by
the Asahi Newspaper – between Tokyo
and London was made, but with a
Mitsubishi aircraft, not with a Fokker.
Just a designer's error, or were we
unable to grasp the real meaning of the
design?

[1] www.famousdiamonds.tripod.com
/cullinandiamonds

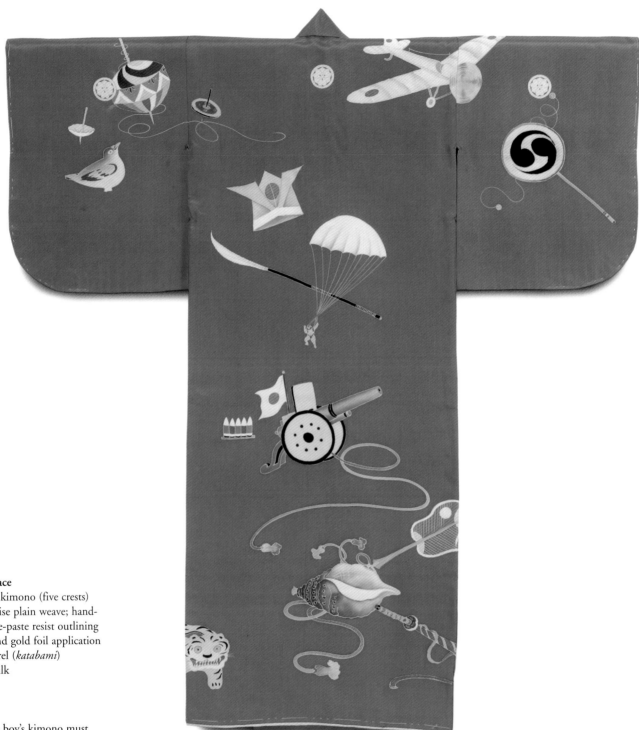

98. War and Peace
Boy's *miyamairi* kimono (five crests)
Outside: turquoise plain weave; hand-painted with rice-paste resist outlining (*yūzen*), silver and gold foil application
Crest: wood sorrel (*katabami*)
Lining: yellow silk
86 × 82 cm
1930–40

This remarkable boy's kimono must have been made in the 1930s, during the optimistic atmosphere of rising militarism, but before the brute realities of warfare were felt. In the 1940s, wearing luxury silk clothing was no longer permitted.
Against a brilliant turquoise background a variety of traditional toys take turns with war motifs: a tank next to a cuddly toy tiger, a hobby horse and a cannon, spinning tops and a parachutist. The painting was made in wonderful colours and with delicate shading. On the front, many motifs have silver outlines and the war-drum shows gold foil application.

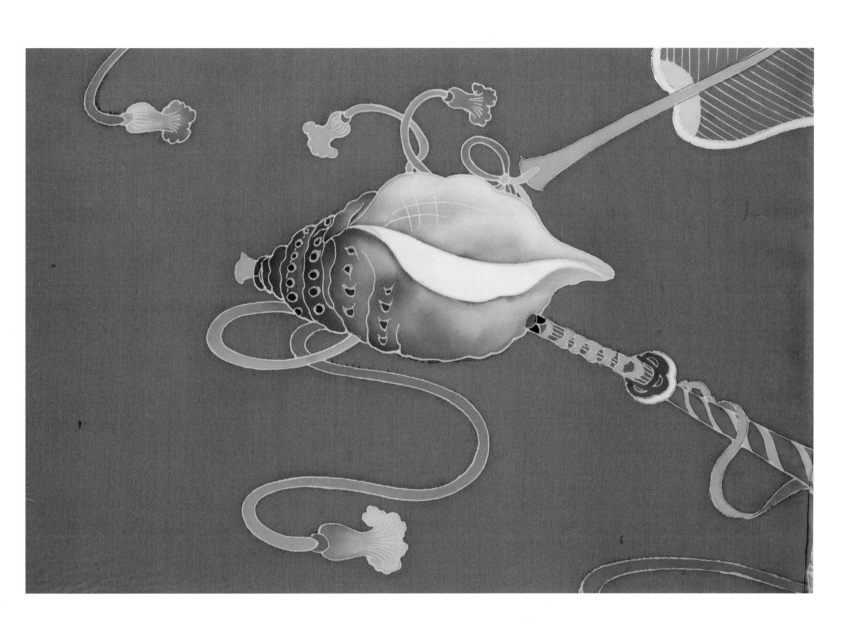

Indigo
The Working Class Colour

A colour for the aristocracy during the Nara period (710–794), natural indigo became more widely available with the advent of vat dyeing (*tatezome*) in the fourteenth century. However, it was the introduction of the cotton culture in the seventeenth century that made indigo popular among the common people. Cotton soon became the most commonly used fabric for large segments of the population, and indigo was a perfect fast dye for it. During the early twentieth century indigo kimono became working class garments, both in the big cities and in rural areas (fig. 43).

Natural indigo can be extracted from a variety of *indigofera* plants (plants that contain indigotine). Its production by fermentation is a laborious and magical process. In the rural areas of Japan it was only done in certain households. During the Tokugawa period, regional styles of indigo fabrics developed: the small provincial towns of Narumi and Arimatsu on the Tōkaidō Road specialised in indigo *shibori*, whereas the castle town Kurume on the southern island of Kyūshū was famous for its indigo *ikat* cloth (*kasuri*). Cat. 101

and 102 were made in Tōhoku, an area in northern Honshū.

Natural indigo or *ai* comprises a variety of hues depending on the number of dye baths: they range from pale blue to violet-back with a metallic sheen. Because of the time-consuming process required to dye the cloth, a search for chemical production began in the nineteenth century. A major step was the finding of the structural formula of indigo by Adolf von Baeyer (1835–1917) in 1878. It took until 1896 for a research team at BASF in Germany to discover a method for the commercial synthesis, when a thermometer accidentally broke above a vat. The leaked mercury happened to accelerate the crucial transformation of naphthalene into naphthalene anhydride greatly.[1] Soon after, the price of natural indigo on the world market dropped dramatically. In early twentieth-century Japan, the use of natural indigo dye declined rapidly. Chemical indigo set the tone.

[1] Molenaar 1985: 31-34.

43. Errand boys in jackets featuring the shop's name (1910–30). Ikjeld.com

99. Ink cake shop
Man's half-length jacket (*hanten*)
Outside: homespun indigo cotton
with stencilled decoration (*katazome*)
Inside: indigo cotton
117 × 89 cm
ca. 1925

This is a typical half-length workman's coat made of indigo cotton. The best known of these jackets are the firemen's *hanten*, with or without elaborately decorated linings.

In this case the shop name Gyokusendo is written in camouflaged, large square characters on the lower half of the jacket, providing it with a mysterious asymmetrical decoration. The reverse is adorned with the large-size shop sign (sash weight or *fundō*), which is repeated in small dimensions on both lapels. Also on the lapels we find the name Nagashima, probably the shop owner. Gyokusendo was a famous shop for ink cakes in Nara, founded in 1864. Such business *hanten* became a popular advertising medium. Therefore they were often called *rokusha kanban* or 'six-foot-long billboards', since six feet of fabric was required to make the coat.

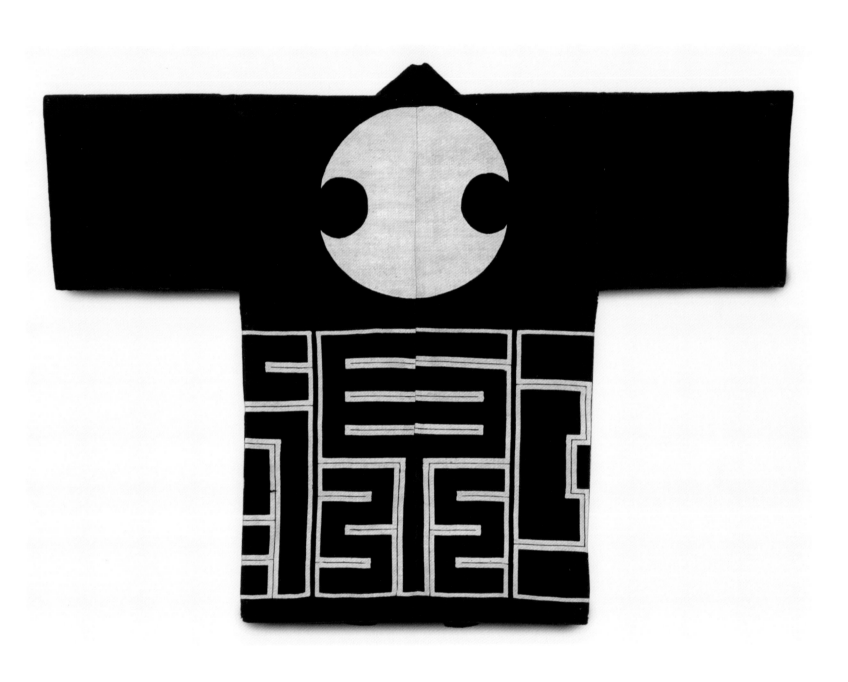

100. Snow
Boy's kimono
Outside: homespun indigo cotton;
plain weave with double *ikat* decoration
(*kasuri*)
Lining: homespun, plain weave cotton
111 × 98 cm
1900–10

It is not difficult to imagine a child
dressed in this Meiji period kimono
running in the snow, which is rendered
on the kimono in double *ikat*. *Ikat* or
kasuri was brought to Japan from the
Ryūkyū Islands in the fourteenth or
fifteenth century. It is one of the *saki-
zome* techniques, because the designs
were applied on the warp and weft
threads before weaving. Small bundles
of several warp and/or weft threads
were wrapped with cotton thread or
fibre before putting them into the dye
bath. The wrapped parts preserved their
natural colour. Once woven into a
fabric, the design became somewhat
blurred due to slight shifting of the
threads (see detail)

Postcard of a young boy in double-*ikat*
kimono. Author's collection

101. Tortoise motif
Man's kimono
Outside: homespun indigo cotton;
plain weave with tie-dye decoration
(*shibori*)
Lining: homespun plain weave indigo
cotton
129 × 122 cm
1900–20

This is a farmer's working garment
(*noragi kimono*) from the Tōhoku
district in northern Japan. The
hexagonal pattern is derived from the
shell of a turtle. The fact that the
sleeves are completely attached to the
body indicates that it is a man's
garment.

102. Maple leaves
Woman's kimono
Outside: homespun indigo cotton;
plain weave with tie-dye decoration
(*shibori*)
Lining: homespun plain weave indigo
cotton
135 × 121 cm
1910–30

Another peasant's kimono from
Tōhoku. The various *shibori* techniques
produce an attractive texture and
decoration. In contrast to *kasuri*, *shibori*
is one of the *ato-zome* techniques, since
the design was applied after the
weaving.
The outlines of the leaves were stitched
and the threads drawn up. The small
white leaves were capped during the
whole dyeing process, whereas the
surface of the maple leaves was further
treated with additional tie-dye.

Sashes
Brocades from Nishijin

Kyoto weaving is as old as the city itself (founded in 794). However, during the Ōnin War (1467–77) the weavers had to seek shelter elsewhere, one destination being Sakai, a major port town. Contacts with Ming China resulted in the adoption of technical innovations. After the war, the weavers returned to the capital and settled in the Nishijin quarter, which became particularly famous for its brocades and other multicoloured patterned weaves (*nishiki*). Such luxury fabrics were used for bridal kimono, *nō* costumes, mountings for paintings, sashes, etc.

Sashes or *obi* only began to play a significant role in the Tokugawa period. Until that time formal and ceremonial dress required loose trousers (*hakama*) over the *kosode* ('small sleeves' kimono). *Hakama* were tied at the waist with a simple cord. During the Tokugawa period, however, such loose trousers went out of fashion, so creating space for the gradual development of opulent sashes. By 1800, women's *maru obi* had reached the extreme dimensions of 30 cm wide and 4 metres long. Therefore it is not surprising that at this point the *obi* became as important an element in formal dress as the *kosode* itself.

At the start of the twentieth century, the *maru obi* was still the foremost ceremonial and formal type of sash, as well as being the most expensive one (cat. 103–111). Due to its length and the stiffener inside, it was very bulky. *Maru obi* were made from a double-width piece of brocade, which was folded over the stiffener. Therefore only one length was sewn.

The *fukuro obi* had almost the same dimensions, but did not contain a stiffener (cat. 118b). It was only patterned on sixty percent of one side. Consequently, this type of sash was less bulky and not reversible. Since it was made from two pieces of cloth, *fukuro obi* were stitched along both long sides.

Nagoya obi were a little shorter than the previous two types (cat. 113). About one third of its length had the same width as the previous types, but the remainder was sewn into half the width of the *fukuro obi*. The wide part was used for folding into the square *taiko* cushion on the back (fig. 47). *Nagoya obi* were easier to handle when dressing and more comfortable to wear.

The *hanhaba obi* had the same length, but only half the width (cat. 114).

Men's sashes were much narrower and have changed little over the centuries. They came either as stiff, thickly woven fabrics about 9 cm wide, which were tied in a half bow (*kaku obi* – cat. 115), or as 25–50 cm wide soft pieces of silk (often tie-dyed), which were folded into a narrow band that used to be worn just under the waist (*heko obi*).

Brocade is a thick multicoloured weave, often including silver and gold thread (*nishiki*). Although it makes the impression of embroidery, brocade is woven with supplementary weft (fig. 44). The introduction of the jacquard loom in the late nineteenth century greatly expanded the possibilities of weaving intricate designs in multiple colours. The manufacturer played the central role in the production of *obi*. He was the pivot in a network of

44. Magnification of brocade *nishiki* weaving

45. Design sketch for a sash with
a Heian period ox-card.
Author's collection

46. Design drawing for a sash with
karabana or 'Chinese flowers'.
The pattern of small squares in the
paper indicates where the holes would
be punched in the jacquard card.
Author's collection

47. Lady's *obi* were tied on the back
in the shape of a square cushion (*taiko*).
Postcard, author's collection

帝國美術院第十二回美術展覽會出品

鹿木子孟郎氏筆   マドモアゼルキタ

Melle K. Kita.

Miss Japan 1931

craftsmen who all depended on him but worked
individually. First the manufacturer ordered a draft sketch
(fig. 45). After approval, the fully detailed design (*zuan*)
was prepared in the standard width of 30 cm and a
variable length of 50–150 cm, depending on the size of
the pattern (fig. 46). The next step was the translation of
the *zuan* into the punch cards for the jacquard loom.
Subsequently, the manufacturer ordered the silk threads in
the required colours from the dyer. Another craftsman
arranged the warp on the loom at an even amount of
tension. Then the weaver could start his work on the
hand-loom that was hired from the manufacturer (the
chinbata system) (fig. 48). First he made one length of the
design for approval by the manufacturer; after that the
complete *obi* could be woven. Wholesalers bought *obi*
from the manufacturers and took care of the distribution
in the city and all-over the country. Since *obi* were luxury
items, their manufacture has always been extremely
vulnerable to economic depression and war.[1]

The *obi* often interrupted the design of a kimono.
Therefore special attention was given to the tasteful
combination of motifs and colours. Compared to the
Meiji period, patterns on Taishō *obi* were much larger.
The geometry of *karabana* or Chinese flowers probably
appealed as the result of the influence in Art Deco, but
the traditional subjects of birds, trees and flowers
remained the most popular.

[1] Hareven 2002.

48. Weaver making an *obi*.
Author's collection

103. Plovers skimming the waves
Woman's *maru obi*
Brocade-woven silk (*nishiki*)
418 × 33 cm
1890–1910

Most *obi* manufactured during the Meiji-period had small patterns and were woven from very fine silk and gold thread in subdued colours, as can be observed on this example.

104. A flowering Paulownia
Woman's *maru obi*
Brocade-woven silk (*nishiki*)
418 × 33 cm
1900–20

Although the design actually consists
of repeating patterns, the result is
a single paulownia tree in blossom,
four metres tall.

105. *Shippō-tsunagi* **motif**
Woman's *maru obi*
Brocade-woven silk (*nishiki*)
418 × 33 cm
1910–20

The *shippō-tsunagi* motif of interlocking circles was brought to Japan from China on lacquerware and cloisonné. The origin, however, seems to lie in ancient Egypt. The gold inner sarcophagus of Tutankhamon was already engraved with *shippō-tsunagi*. This motif on a sarcophagus is no coincidence, since cat's mummies from the same burial chamber were enveloped in nets of cylindrical beads – the cords being tied into knots between every bead – resulting in the motif of the *obi* (but yet without the small floral lozenges called *hanabishi*). These beaded nets seem to be the real origin of the motif, which subsequently spread, first to Byzantium (probably with the proto-cloisonné from Egypt), then to the Middle East and China via the Silk Road, and finally all over the world.

106. Pines shoots, cones and needles
Woman's *maru obi*
Brocade-woven silk (*nishiki*)
398 × 28 cm
1910–20

The pine tree was considered a symbol
of strength, and a good omen for a long
life. Its pointed needles were believed to
chase away evil spirits.
On this *obi* the young pines, cones and
needles are seen from above in a golden
light, possibly an influence from the
new Nihonga painting style at the
beginning of the twentieth century.
Unlike most other *maru obi*, this
example lacks the stiffener inside.

107. A garden in bloom
Woman's *maru obi*
Brocade-woven silk (*nishiki*)
390 × 32 cm
1920–40

In addition to the Three Friends (pine, plum and bamboo), various kinds of chrysanthemums, vine and a white-flowering herb can be observed. Characteristic of this period is the alternation of a large element in blue and violet respectively, as seen here in the chrysanthemums. This type of alternation created greater variety in the repetition of the patterns produced by the jacquard loom.

108. *Hagoromo*
Woman's *maru obi*
Brocade-woven silk (*nishiki*)
405 × 32 cm
1920–40

The story of a mortal who stole an angel's cloak and so prevented her return to heaven exists in many cultures. *Hagoromo* is the Japanese version and the subject of a famous *nō* play by Zeami (1363–1443).
The breaking waves indicate the beach. The feathered cloak in the shape of a butterfly and the oversize headgear with a large *hōō* on top of it are hanging in the pine tree, which is almost entirely covered by such profusion. Two fans complete the motif.

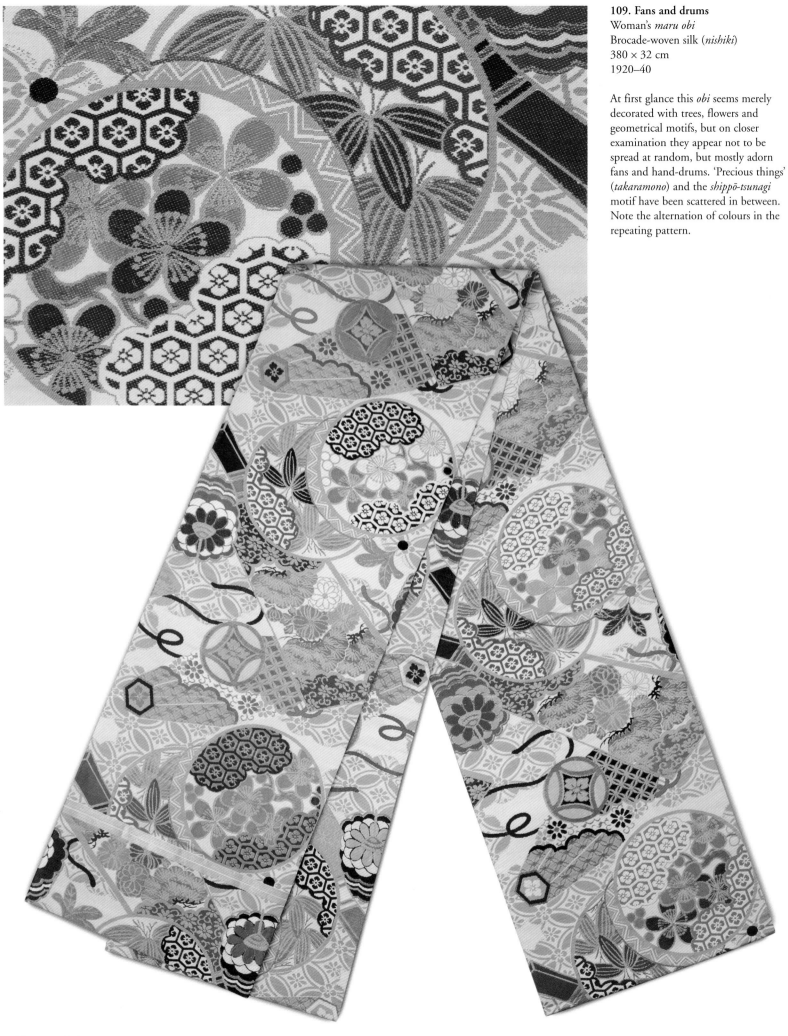

109. Fans and drums

Woman's *maru obi*
Brocade-woven silk (*nishiki*)
380 × 32 cm
1920–40

At first glance this *obi* seems merely decorated with trees, flowers and geometrical motifs, but on closer examination they appear not to be spread at random, but mostly adorn fans and hand-drums. 'Precious things' (*takaramono*) and the *shippō-tsunagi* motif have been scattered in between. Note the alternation of colours in the repeating pattern.

110. White peacock
Woman's *maru obi*
Brocade-woven silk (*nishiki*)
396 × 31 cm
1920–40

Maru obi were being worn in the so-called *taiko* style with a square fold on the back (fig. 47). This style had nothing to do with the hand drum or *taiko*, but the term was derived from the Taikobashi, a bridge in Tokyo opened in 1823. On that occasion geisha created a stir with the new way they had their *obi* tied.

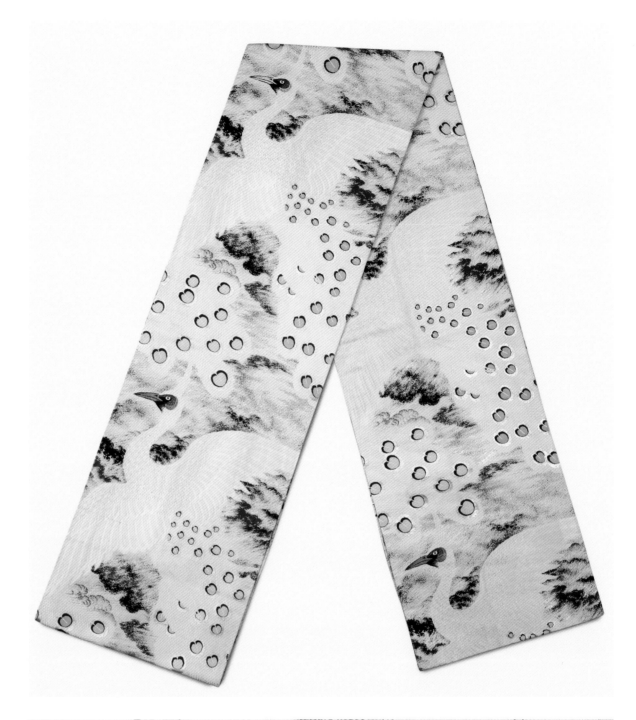

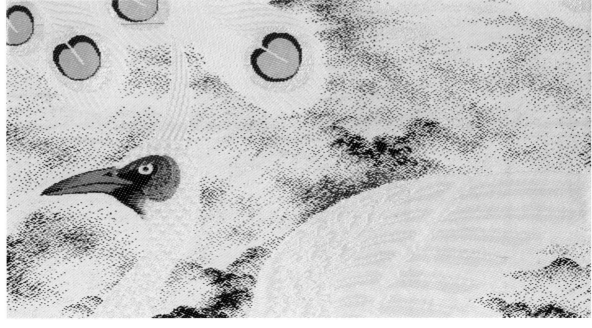

111. Rimpa fans

Woman's *maru obi*
'Nail' tapestry weave (*tsume tsuzure*)
410 × 30 cm
1920–40

The Rimpa style originated in the seventeenth century. The painters and designers Hon'ami Kōetsu (1558–1637) and Ogata Kōrin (1658–1716) had created this two-dimensional style. Rimpa experienced several revivals, amongst others at the beginning of the twentieth century. The abbreviated flower and plant motifs, which adorn the fans on this *obi*, are exemplary of the decorative style.

The exceptional *tsume tsuzure* technique, applied to produce this *obi*, made use of a number of differently coloured weft threads, each of which went to and fro to entirely cover the warp in a certain area. Each colour is separated from the neighbouring one by small slits (like in *kilim* tapestry) (see detail). The word *tsume* means 'nail', and refers to the jagged fingernails, which pressed the thin weft threads tight (see illustration). The saw-tooth shape of the nails was achieved by filing. It goes without saying that the *tsume tsuzure* technique was extremely time-consuming.

Slits separating the colours in the fabric

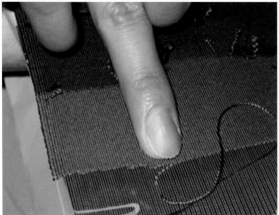

Saw-tooth shape of a fingernail

112. Mandarin ducks
Woman's *maru obi*
Brocade-woven silk (*nishiki*)
392 × 32 cm
1920–40

A pair of mandarin ducks rests by a stream. They symbolise conjugal love, faithfulness and happiness. Under the gnarled old pine tree, a flowering plum and bamboo are growing, so completing the *shōchikubai* emblem of a lucky triad.
The production of an obi required the cooperation of several craftsmen, among them the dyer of the silk threads. One can imagine how important the skills of the dye workshop (*someya*) must have been for the manufacture of a colourful *obi* like this.

113. Drum and flute
Woman's *Nagoya obi*
Ivory plain weave silk with embroidery
336 × 31 cm
1920–40

Like several other novelties in Japanese
fashion, the *Nagoya obi* was introduced
by geisha. A 1920s invention of a
Nagoya seamstress, these less bulky *obi*
became popular among geisha for
informal daytime occasions. The torso-
wrapping portion is only half the width
of the part that was meant to be tied
into the *taiko* on the back.
In this *obi* there is a pun on the word
taiko. It is not only the name of the
square bulky cushion in which the *obi*
is being folded but also the word for
drum.
The sophisticated embroidery creates
an interesting relief in the textile – for
example in the cords and tassels.

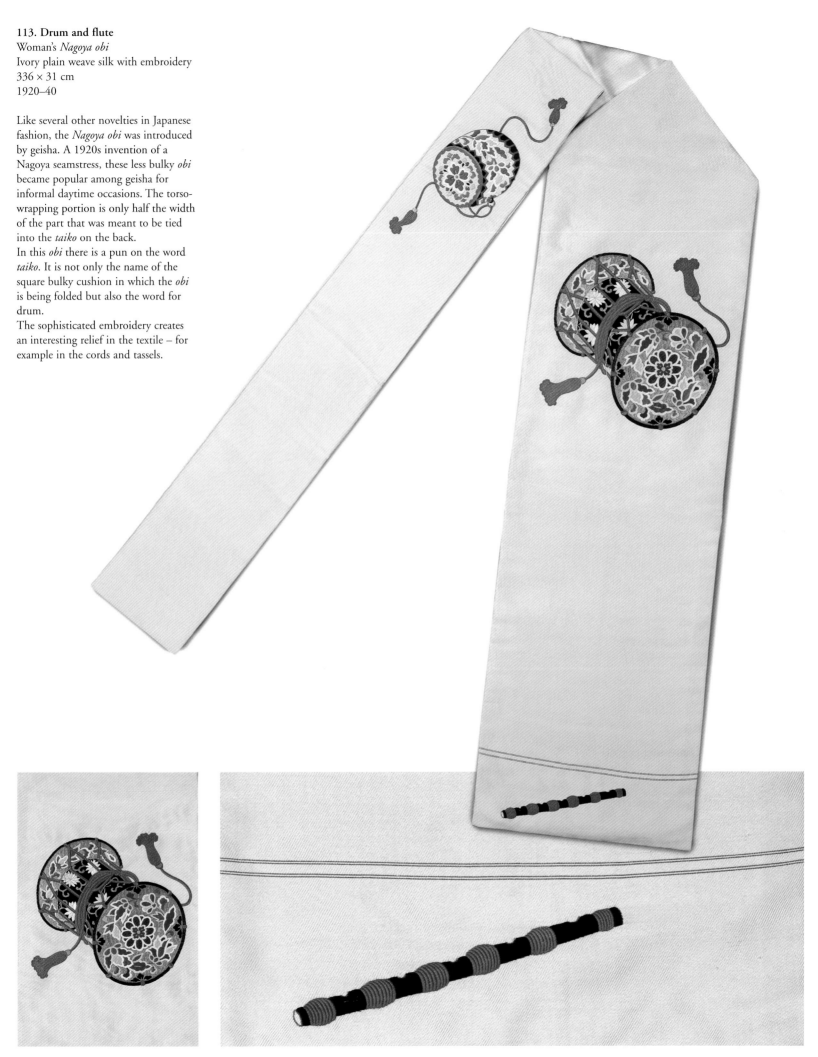

114. Chinese flowers
Woman's *hanhaba obi*
Brocade-woven silk (*nishiki*)
308 × 16 cm
1920–40

Karabana (imaginary Chinese flowers) were popular motifs for *obi* both before and after World War II. They were often octagonal or star-shaped. The colour combination of blue, purple and yellow is often seen in sashes from the interwar years. The half-width *hanhaba obi* was considered casual dress. During the early Tokugawa period, the sash was still narrow or nothing more than a cord. It was only in the nineteenth century that the *obi* developed to its present extreme size.

115. Man's *obi*
Brocade-woven silk (*nishiki*)
375 × 8 cm
1920–40

This reversible *kaku obi* has an abstract pattern with a central band of pseudo-calligraphy on one side. Such narrow *obi* were practical for carrying all kinds of personal utensils, such as purses, tobacco pouches and medicine containers, which dangled from silk cords attached to a *netsuke*. Traditional Japanese dress had no pockets. Therefore men used to wear *sagemono* to allow utensils to dangle from the sash, whereas ladies used to tuck things away behind their wide *obi* or put them in their long sleeves.

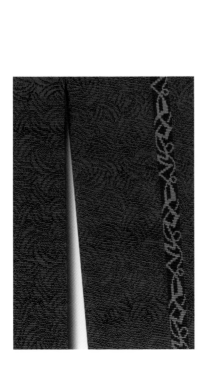

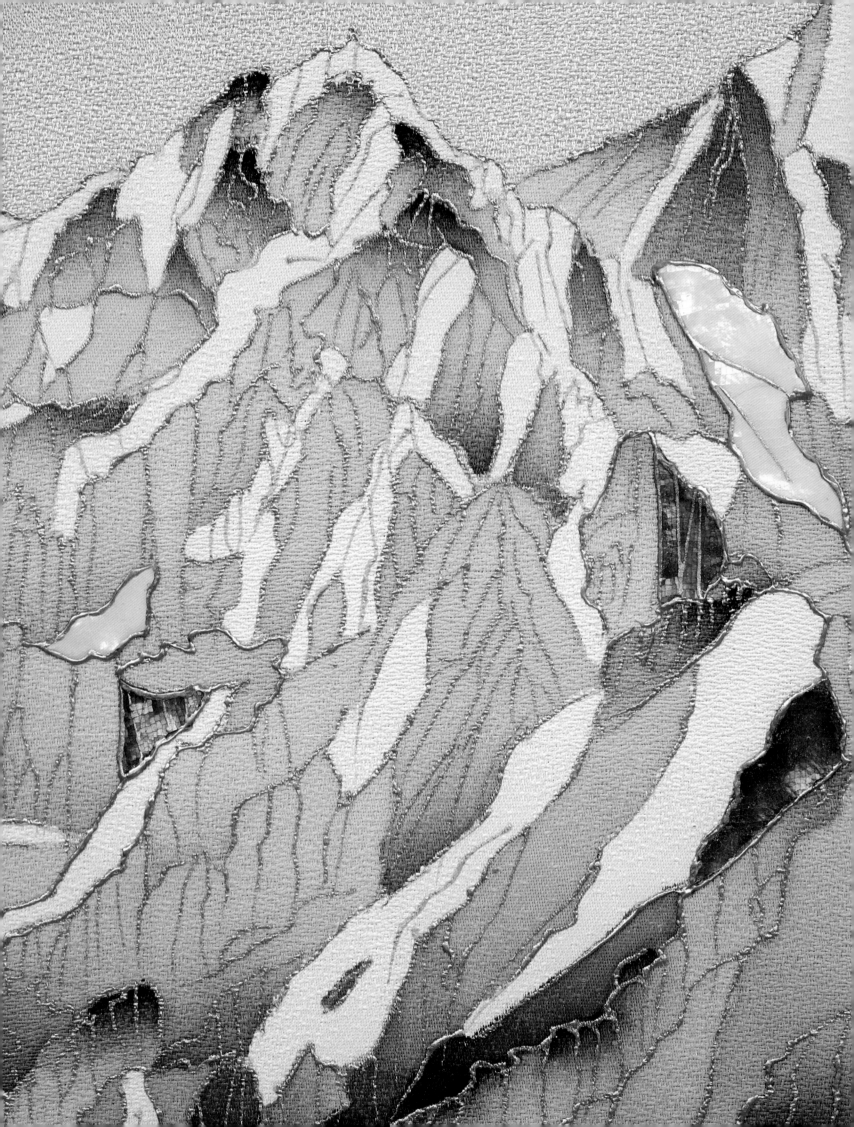

Post-war Kimono

Kimono production was almost entirely interrupted during World War II. After the war, Japan declared that it would turn itself into a nation to be respected for its culture rather than for its power. This intention initially favoured traditional aesthetics. The variety of kimono models decreased and kimono were mainly worn as a single layer garment stiffly wrapped around the body. Increasing affluence in the 1960s stimulated demand, which in turn gave impetus to new artistry and a (last?) revival of the kimono industry. The 1964 Olympic Games in Tokyo are often regarded as the time that Japan felt fully accepted again by the international community. To some extent the kimono regained its position as Japan's national dress. Most women own a few kimono, but only wear them on ceremonial occasions.

Apart from objects of fashion, kimono have also become objects of art. The annual Exhibition of Traditional Art Crafts always includes a kimono section, and the Tokyo National University of Fine Arts and Music has a training programme for textile dyeing and weaving.

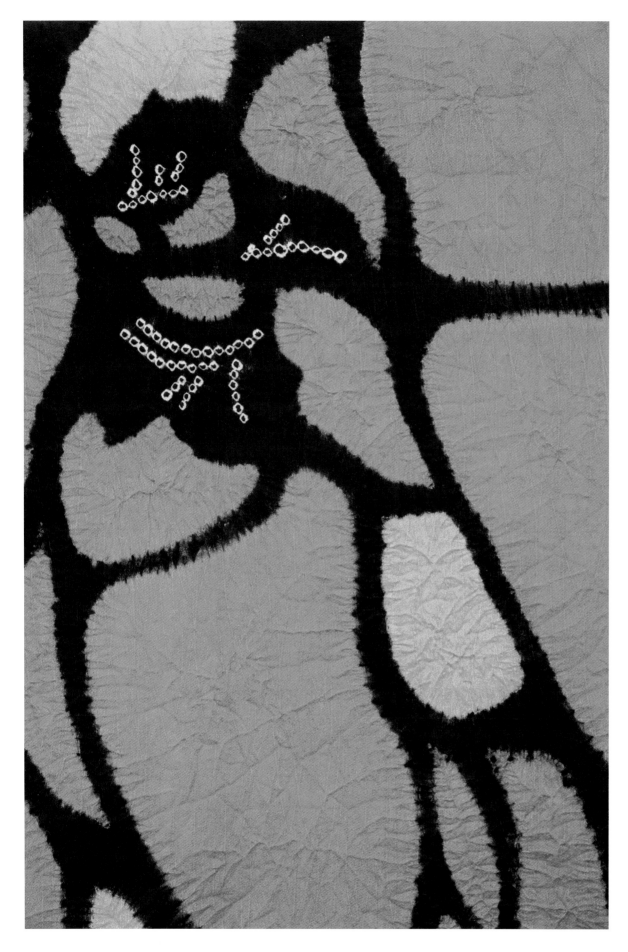

116. Abstract pattern
Woman's *haori* (no crests)
Outside: fine crepe silk (*kinsha*);
damask weave (*rinzu*) with tie-dye
decoration (*shibori*)
Lining: white silk; plain weave with
stencil-printed decoration
132 × 86 cm
1960–80

The large tie-dyed areas provide this
jacket with a wrinkled texture, which is
further enhanced by the hardly visible
patterning of criss-cross lines in the fine
crepe silk (*rinzu*). Utensils for the tea
ceremony adorn the lining.

117. Flying goose
Woman's kimono (no crests)
Outside: black crepe silk (*chirimen*),
dyed and embroidered
Lining: white silk
159 × 125 cm
1950–70

The goose is embroidered in alternating
short and long stitches (*sashi-nui*). The
fact that the curved lines of the
background were 'hand-drawn' – but
actually woven – adds much to the
appeal of this kimono.

118. Alpine scenery and a lakeside castle
Set of a woman's *hōmongi* and *obi*

118a. Woman's *hōmongi* (one crest)
Outside: pink fine crepe silk (*kinsha*),
damask weave (*rinzu*); hand-painted
with rice-paste resist outlining (*yūzen*);
all white outlines are covered in gold
relief with a resin-like material; mother-
of-pearl application
Signatures: 'Taizō' with seal and 'Yōko'
Crest: 'comma shapes' (*tomoe*)
Lining: white silk

174 × 142 cm
1980–2000

Surrounded by forests and fields, the
small town nestles in the valley. The
tiled roofs of the houses suggest a
European location, perhaps somewhere
in the Alps or northern Italy. A ridge of
high mountains can be seen in the far
distance, their peaks covered with snow.
This contemporary kimono has been
meticulously dyed in the *yūzen*
technique. In this case the dyer did not
use gold foil to cover the remaining

white lines, but a resin-like material,
that lies like thick gold lines on the
textile. Not only the white outlines
have been traced, but all kinds of
details have been accentuated in this
manner. This provides the decoration
with a remarkably tactile aspect.
Another striking technique is the inlay
of both blue-green and white mother-
of-pearl in many places of the
decoration.
The silk itself shows small horizontally
oriented clouds woven into the fabric
(*rinzu*). Because of the densely dyed

design at the lower end, these clouds
are only noticeable in the plain pink
part of the kimono, which is thereby
transformed into the sky.
The kimono is signed: Taizō and a seal.
The same name has been woven into
the silk lining. In addition, the name
Yōko is inscribed in the gold resin-like
material, which may suggest a second
craftsperson, who did this part of the
decoration, or perhaps the owner.

118b. Woman's *fukuro obi*
Hand-painted, rice-paste resist
outlining (*yūzen*); all white outlines are
covered in gold relief with a resin-like
material; mother-of-pearl application
Signature: 'Taizō' with seal
432 × 31 cm
1980–2000

The matching *obi* features a fortified
castle with four battlemented towers at
the corners. The castle sits on a wooded
hill and overlooks a lake.
The techniques are similar to those
applied on the kimono, but with the
addition of a background of large gold
and silver spots. Like all *fukuro obi* the
decoration covers only part of the
surface.

Bibliography

Art Deco and the Orient: 1920s-1930s – Longing for Paris (exh. cat. with Japanese and English text). Tokyo: Tokyo Metropolitan Foundation for History and Culture, 2000.

Asai Chū (exh. cat. – Japanese text). Sakura: Sakura City Museum of Art, 2003.

Atkins, Jacqueline M. (editor). *Wearing Propaganda. Textiles on the Home Front in Japan, Britain, and the United States, 1931–1945*. New Haven and London: Yale University Press, 2005.

Bix, Herbert P., *Hirohito and the Making of Modern Japan*. New York: Harper-Collins Publishers, 2001.

Boersma, Foekje. *Op de keeper beschouwd. Handboek voor het behoud van textielcollecties*. Amsterdam: Stichting Textielcommissie Nederland, 2000.

Crafts Reforming in Kyoto [1910–1940]. A Struggle between Tradition and Renovation (exh. cat. with Japanese and English text, but essays in Japanese only). Kyoto: The National Museum of Modern Art, 1998.

Daalen, J. van. *Blumen und Pflanzen im Kunstgewerbe Ostasiens*. Cologne: Kunsthaus am Museum, 1978.

Dalby, Liza. *Geisha*. Berkeley, Los Angeles, London: University of California Press, 1998.

Dalby, Liza. *Kimono. Fashioning Culture*. Seattle and London: University of Washington Press, 2001.

Dees, Jan. *Facing Modern Times. The Revival of Japanese Lacquer Art 1890–1950*. Doctoral thesis, Leiden 2007.

Dower, John. *The Elements of Japanese Design. A Handbook of Family Crests, Heraldry & Symbolism*. Boston, London: Weatherhill, 2005.

Edmunds, Will. H. *Pointers and Clues to the Subjects of Chinese and Japanese Art*. Chicago: Art Media Resources, n.d. (original publication from 1934).

Emery, Irene. *The Primary Structures of Fabrics. An Illustrated Classification*. Washington D.C.: The Textile Museum, 1994.

Fujii, Kenzō. *Japanese Modern Textiles (Kyoto Shoin's Art Library of Japanese Textiles Vol. 17)*. Kyoto: Kyoto Shoin Co., 1993.

Godoy, George R., '*Obi Zuan*. Japan's Unseen Paintings'. In *Arts of Asia*, vol. 36/4 (2006), 62-71.

Hareven, Tamara K. *The Silk Weavers of Kyoto. Family and Work in a Changing Traditional Industry*. Berkeley, Los Angeles, London: University of California Press, 2002.

Iwasaki, Mineko and Rande Brown. *Geisha of Gion*. London: Pocket Books, 2003.

Jansen, Marius B. *The Making of Modern Japan*. Cambridge (MA), London: The Belknap Press of Harvard University Press, 2000.

Japanese Family Crests (Japanese text). Seigensha 2006.

Joly, Henri L. *Legend in Japanese Art*. Rutland (VT), Tokyo: Charles E. Tuttle Co., 1967 (original publication from 1908).

Kamisaka Sekka: Rimpa Master – Pioneer of Modern Design (exh. cat.). The National Museum of Modern Art/Birmingham Museum of Art/The Asahi Shimbun, Kyoto/Alabama 2003.

Kashiwagi, Hiroshi. 'Design and War. Kimono as "Parlor Performance" Propaganda'. In *Wearing Propaganda* (ed. Jacqueline M. Atkins). New Haven and London: Yale University Press, 2005.

Kodansha Encyclopedia of Japan. Tokyo: Kodansha, 1999.

Large, Stephen S. *Emperors of the Rising Sun. Three Biographies*. Tokyo: Kodansha, 1997.

Maruyama, Nobuhiki. *Yūzen Dyeing (Kyoto Shoin's Art Library of Japanese Textiles Vol. 5)*. Kyoto: Kyoto Shoin Co., 1993.

McCullough, Helen Craig. *Yoshitsune. A Fifteenth-Century Japanese Chronicle*. Palo Alto (CA): Stanford University Press, 1971.

Milhaupt, Teri Satsuki. 'Facets of the Kimono: Reflections of Japan's Modernity'. In *Arts of Japan. The John C. Weber Collection*. Berlin: Museum für Ostasiatische Kunst, 2006.

Moes, Robert. *Mingei. Japanese Folk Art*. New York: Universe Books, 1985.

Molenaar, Leo. 'De indigosynthese. Produkt van wetenschap en chemische industrie'. In *Indigo. Leven in een kleur* (ed.: Loan Oei). Weesp: Fibula-Van Dishoeck, 1985.

Morris, Ivan (trans.). *The Pillow Book of Sei Shōnagon*. Harmondsworth: Penguin Books, 1967.

Oei, Loan (ed.). *Indigo. Leven in een kleur*. Weesp: Fibula-Van Dishoeck, 1985.

Okamura, Kichiemon. *Japanese Ikat. (Kyoto Shoin's Art Library of Japanese Textiles Vol. 12)*. Kyoto: Kyoto Shoin Co., 1993.

Rodd, Laurel Resplica (trans.). *Kokinshū. A Collection of Poems, Ancient and Modern.* Boston: Cheng & Tsui Company, 2004.

Sashiko Hanten Fireman's Coat. The Kuwata Collection. Kyoto: Kyoto Shoin, 1997.

Sapin, Julia. 'Merchandising Art and Identity in Meiji Japan: Kyoto *Nihonga* Artists' Designs for Takashimaya Department Store, 1868–1912'. In *Journal of Design History* vol. 17 no.4 (2004): 317-36.

Sato, Barbara. *The New Japanese Woman. Modernity, Media, and Women in Interwar Japan.* Durham (NC), London: Duke University Press, 2003.

Seidensticker, Edward. *Low City, High City. Tokyo from Edo to the Earthquake.* Rutland (VT), Tokyo: Charles E. Tuttle Company, 1984.

Seidensticker, Edward. *Tokyo Rising. The City since the Great Earthquake.* Cambridge (MA): Harvard University Press, 1991.

Shibori. The Inventive Art of Japanese Shaped Resist Dyeing. Tradition. Techniques. Innovation, by Yoshiko Iwamoto Wada, Mary Kellogg Rice and Jane Barton. Tokyo, New York, London: Kodansha International, 1999.

Sunagawa, Akira. 'Introduction to Hikeshi Sashiko Hanten'. In *Daruma,* no. 19 (1998): 20-32.

Taishō Chic: Japanese Modernity, Nostalgia and Deco (published in conjunction with the exhibition of the same title). Honolulu (HI): Honolulu Academy of Arts, 2001.

Tipton, Elise and John Clark (eds.). *Being Modern in Japan. Culture and Society from the 1910s to the 1930s.* Honolulu (HI): University of Hawai'i Press, 2000.

Tuer, Andrew W. *Japanese Stencil Designs.* New York: Dover Publications, 1967.

Van Assche, Annie. '*Meisen* – Early 20th Century Fashion Kimono'. In *Daruma,* no. 22 (1999): 30-39.

Van Assche, Annie (ed.). *Fashioning Kimono. Dress and Modernity in Early Twentieth Century Japan.* Milan: 5 Continents, 2005.

Volker, T. *The Animal in Far Eastern Art.* Leiden: E.J. Brill, 1975.

Volker, T. 'Some Notes on Japanese Stencil Makers'. In *Andon,* no. 16 (1984): 7-11.

Wakakuwa, Midori. 'War-Promoting Kimono (1931–1945)'. In *Wearing Propaganda. Textiles on the Home Front in Japan, Britain and the United States 1931–1945.* New Haven (VT), London: Yale University Press, 2005.

Waley, Paul. *Tokyo Now and Then. An Explorer's Guide.* New York, Tokyo: Weatherhill, 1984.

Warth, Terry. 'Evolution of the Japanese *Haori*'. In *Arts of Asia,* vol. 36/4 (2006): 47-61.

Weber, V.-F. *"Koji Hōten". Dictionnaire a l'usage des amateurs et collectionneurs d'objects d'art Japonais et Chinois.* New York: Hacker Art Books, 1965 (2 vols.).

Yang, Sunny and Rochelle M. Narasin. *Textile Art of Japan.* Tokyo: Shufunotomo, 1989.

Zijde en Kunstzijde. Textielcommissie Musea, 1992.

Glossary

Abuna-e: risqué

Ai: indigo

Asa: hemp cloth

Ato-zome: pattern dyeing after weaving

Bijinga: pictures of beautiful women

Chinbata: hired looms

Chirimen: crepe silk

Fudangi: everyday wear

Fukuro obi: pocket sash for women

Furisode: formal kimono with 'swinging sleeves' for unmarried young women

Futo-ori: thick weave

Habutae: thick glossy plain weave silk

Hakama: loose trousers

Han'eri: detachable collar

Hanhaba obi: half-width sash

Hanten: half-length jacket

Haori: jacket

Haregi: formal and ceremonial wear

Heiyō-moyō: warp and weft patterned *meisen* fabric

Heko obi: men's sash made of soft silk

Hinagata: pattern

Hinagata-bon: kimono pattern book

Hira-nui: flat-stitch embroidery

Hogushi-moyō: warp patterned *meisen* fabric

Hōmongi: visiting wear

Irotomesode: coloured formal kimono for married women

Jūni-hitoe: twelve-layered women's dress worn in the Heian period

Kabuki: popular drama on historical and domestic themes originating in the 17th century

Kachō: flower and bird

Kaku obi: brocade men's obi

Kaoike: shell game

Karabana: Chinese flowers

Karsashishi: Chinese lion

Karinui: kimono temporarily sewn for display

Kasuri: ikat

Katagami: impregnated paper stencils

Kata-yūzen: stencil-printing with a mixture of pigments and rice paste

Katazome: stencil dyeing

Kimono: 'thing to wear'

Kinsha: fine crepe silk

Kiribame: patchwork

Kosode: small-sleeved woman's dress

Kurotomesode: black formal kimono for married women

Maru obi: the most formal and bulky brocade sash for women

Meisen: taffeta-like silk with ikat imitation

Meisho: famous place

Mimasu-mon: crest of three nesting rice measures

Miyamairi: infant's ceremonial kimono for the first visit to the Shinto shrine

Mon: crest

Mompe: baggy trousers worn by working women during WWII

Musō haori: jacket with lining made of the same material as the outside

Nagajuban: under-kimono

Nagoya obi: women's sash consisting of a wide and a narrow part

Nihonga: Japanese-style painting

Nishijin: weaving quarter in Kyoto

Nishiki: brocade weave

Nō: classical drama with actors in opulent dress and wearing masks

Nui: embroidery

Nui mon: embroidered crest

Obi: sash

Omote mon: recto version of the crest

Orimono: woven decorations

Rinzu: damask weave

Ro: gauze weave

Sagara-nui: French-knot embroidery

Saki-zome: pattern dyeing before weaving

Sashi-nui: embroidery with alternating short and long stitches

Sayagata: key-fret pattern

Semamori: stitched charms

Shibori: tie-dye

Shin Hanga: 'new print' developed since 1915

Somemono: dyed decorations

Susohiki: trailing dance kimono for a geisha

Taiko: boxlike pouf in which women's sashes are tied at the back

Tarikubi: court robe in ancient China

Tatezome: vat dyeing

Tegaki-yūzen: freehand painted *yūzen*

Tsukesage: semiformal dress with combined hem and shoulder decoration

Tsume tsuzure: tapestry weave that requires jagged fingernails

Tsumugi: raw silk

Tsutsugaki-yūzen: classical *yūzen* with rice-paste outlining

Uchikake: bridal kimono

Ura mon: verso crest

Urushi: lacquer

Utsushi-nori: a mixture of dyes with rice paste

Wafuku: Japanese dress

Yamabushi: wandering priest

Yōfuku: Western dress

Yokoso-moyō: weft patterned *meisen* fabric

Yukata: cotton kimono worn at home

Yūzen: silk painting techniques that make use of a washable fixative to keep the dyes in place

Zuan: design drawing

Index